Women
in Modern China

Transition, Revolution and Contemporary Times

by
Marjorie Wall Bingham & Susan Hill Gross

Written under **Women In World Area Studies**, an ESEA, Title IV-C Federal Project granted by the Minnesota Department of Education.

Project Co-Directors: Marjorie Wall Bingham and Susan Hill Gross
Project Assistant: Nancy Keyt Wright

GEM
ARY ICCUEN
publications inc.
411 Mallalieu Drive
Hudson, Wisconsin 54016

Photo Credits

Metropolitan Museum of Art 9
Richard Bancroft 19, 24, 28, 85, 86, 88, 93
Gail Mathisen 81, 83, 97a, 97b
Roxanne Witke, *Comrade Chiang Ch'ing* 74
BBC Hulton Picture Library 65
William Rockhill Nelson Gallery of Art 56
Wide World Photos 68b, 75
Lawrence and Wishart, *The Slaves of the Cool Mountains* by Alan Winnington 45
Harry Franck, *Wandering in Northern China* 17, 53
Mary Backus Rankin, *Early Chinese Revolutionaries* 35
Isaac Headland, *Court Life in China* 58
China Reconstructs, July, 1977, 27
China Reconstructs, January, 1976, 57

Acknowledgments

Excerpts from *The Slaves of the Cool Mountains* by Alan Winnington. Reprinted by permission of Lawrence & Wishart, Ltd.

Excerpts from pages 30-32 in *Girl Rebel: The Autobiography of Hsieh Pingying*, translated by Adet and Anor Lin (John Day). Copyright, 1940, by Harper & Row, Publishers, Inc. Reprinted by permission of the Publisher.

"The Chinese Language Today: Romanization" from *China: Yesterday and Today*, Second Edition, edited by Molly Joel Coye and Jon Livingston. Copyright © 1975, 1979 by Bantam Books, Inc. Reprinted by permission of the publisher. All rights reserved.

Chart from *China's Forty Millions* by June Teufel Dreyer, pages 277-278. Reprinted by permission of Harvard University Press.

Selection reprinted from *Daughter of the Khans* by Liang Yen, with the permission of W.W. Norton & Company, Inc. Copyright 1955 by Walter Briggs and Margaret Briggs.

Excerpts from *Fanshen: A Documentary of Revolution in a Chinese Village* by William Hinton. Copyright © 1966 by William Hinton. Reprinted by permission of Monthly Review Press.

Excerpts from *The First Years of a Yangyi Commune* by Isabel and David Crook, 1966. Reprinted by permission of Humanities Press, Inc.

Excerpts from Nym Wales and Kim San, *Song of Ariran: A Korean Community in the Chinese Revolution* (Palo Alto, California: Ramparts Press, 1972), p. 325.

Excerpts from *Feminism and Socialism in China* by Elizabeth Croll. Reprinted by permission of Routledge and Kegan Paul Ltd.

Excerpts from *Flowers in the Mirror* by Li Ju-Chen. Translated from the Chinese by Lin Tai-Yi. Published by the University of California Press and Peter Owen, London.

Women in World Cultures (Women in World Area Studies) is a project of St. Louis Park Independent School District #283 and Robbinsdale Independent School District #281, Title IV:C ESEA. The opinions and other contents of this book do not necessarily reflect the position or policy of the State of Minnesota or the U.S. Government and no official endorsement should be inferred.

Design, illustrations and typography by Richard Scales Advertising, Inc. Minneapolis, Minnesota.

411 Mallalieu Drive • Hudson, Wisconsin 54016

International Standard Book Numbers
0-86596-003-8 Paper Edition
0-86596-028-3 Library Edition

Preface

The authors of *Women in Modern China* wish to acknowledge the special assistance of the following people in preparing this book:

Linda Walton-Vargo, area consultant
Ann Bailey, reader
Sally Hart, reader and language consultant
Nancy Slaughter, traveler's report
Richard Bancroft, photographs
Gail Mathisen, photographs
Hua-yuan Li Mowry, consultant
Rosemary Johnson, editor
Tom Egan, reader
Bert Gross, editor
Mike Cooley, pilot teacher
Tom Crampton, pilot teacher
Marjorie Ferris, pilot teacher
Jerry Gottstein, pilot teacher
Joel Tormoen, pilot teacher

In addition to these individuals, the University of Minnesota Library staff cooperated with time and patience to make research for this book possible.

Table of Contents

Introduction

WOMEN IN WORLD CULTURES is the product of a federally funded grant to develop materials on women for global studies and world history courses. The books are available in both hardback editions for library use and paper editions that may be purchased in sets of multiple copies for the classroom.

This project grew out of a search of resources which showed a clear lack of available materials appropriate for the study of women in other cultures. Women's roles in the history of various areas of the world were not included in usual curriculum and library materials. Women's lives were often subsumed under such titles as "the history of man," "the family," or "exceptional women." There were few attempts to explain or to describe how various classes of women lived at different times in particular cultures.

Cultural values were not analyzed in the context of the position of women. For example, Athens of the 5th century B.C. was usually called the "Golden Age" of Greece. Yet Athenian women had very restricted opportunities and diminished status compared to both earlier and later periods of Greek history. Materials that described Islam and the Arab world usually showed little understanding or acknowledgment of the powerful role that Muslim women often played within their "separate" worlds. In discounting the female half of humanity, the global curricular materials often seriously distorted the history and culture of these world areas.

WOMEN IN WORLD CULTURES has been designed to provide students with some resources for discovering the diversity of women's roles in a variety of world cultures. Each book presents both historical roles of women and information on their contemporary status. A major effort has been made to incorporate primary source materials. Descriptions by women of their own lives have been used whenever possible. Other types of information used include government reports, statistics, anthropologist's data, folklore, and art.

Each classroom unit includes a set of books, one teacher's guide and a sound filmstrip. A glossary of terms and a bibliography in each book aid students investigating an unfamiliar world area. The units are designed to supplement regular course offerings. The ones now available are: *Women in India, Women in the USSR, Women in Islam, Women in Israel, Women in Traditional China, Women in Modern China*. Future units include: *Women in Africa, Women in Latin America, Women in Ancient Greece and Rome, Women in Medieval and Renaissance Europe* and *Women in Modern Europe*.

Each unit has been field tested and revised to meet student and teacher comments. Students have been enthusiastic about the materials. Since these units are mainly centered around people's lives and emphasize social history, they are appealing to young people.

Chapter 1

Women in Transitional China

Chapter Contents

A. The Beginnings of Reform for Women in China 1700-1920

Women in traditional China had played various roles depending on their class, geographic location and time period.[1] Wealthier classes in China had seen women as empresses in power, as poets, educated writers and as artists. Women in the lower classes led more restricted lives, yet aided in the subsistence of their familiies.

Whatever the economic class, there were some issues which applied to women generally. Among these issues were differences in status depending on age. Older women generally received more respect, while younger women might be dominated by other family members. Women were expected to marry and to have sons to carry on family traditions. Daughters were generally less welcome than sons and were expected to obey male relatives. Besides these issues, Chinese women had few property rights, no right to divorce, and no place in the important examination system for government jobs. Although face-veiling was not customary in China, women were expected to stay close to home or even to be secluded. As part of this seclusion, perhaps, the practice of footbinding curtailed women's physical mobility.

The issues concerning Chinese women became important to various groups within China who wanted to see the reform and modernization of China. Often these reformers focused on the issue of footbinding as a symbol of women's rights in China.

The Manchu emperors as early as Shun-Zhi[2] (1644-1662) had tried unsuccessfully to get rid of footbinding by issuing decrees. The custom was so much a part of Chinese society, however, that the Manchus did not wish to risk rebellion by using more forceful methods to end the practice. There were, though, some Chinese men as early as the 18th century who wrote concerning reform for women. Since Chinese women rarely were allowed to speak publicly for themselves, the Chinese "feminist" movement began with male writers.

1. For a wider treatment of women in traditional China, see Gross and Bingham, *WOMEN IN TRADITIONAL CHINA*.
2. Please note that in the case of certain famous historical personages no attempt has been made to change the romanization of their names as it was felt such changes would create confusion rather than clarify pronunciation. **Pinyin is used throughout *Women in Modern China* except in the case of a few tribal or minority names. An explanation of Pinyin appears on pages 104 to 106.**

These writers, like You Zhengxie (1775-1840) and Yuan Mei (1716-1799)[3] did not rebel against Confucian ideals; they still stressed the importance of motherhood and family. But they did protest against several practices which they claimed came into Chinese society over the centuries. Particularly they protested against footbinding which they saw as unnatural and physically harmful. While they still upheld the ideal of chastity for single women, they stressed the unfairness of widows not being allowed to remarry. Yuan Mei especially thought women's intellectual abilities should be used. He encouraged several women as his "pupils" in their poetry writing and saw to it that their poetry was published. There was considerable opposition to this publishing. One of his critics wrote:

"...Most of the ladies in rich families south of the Jiangze have been led astray by him. They publish their manuscripts of poems and get a lot of publicity for themselves, in total disregard of the separation between men and women and almost forgetting that they are females. These ladies do not cultivate the proper culture of women; how can they ever have any really poetic talent?..." [4]

Other writers, however, also supported the need for reform. One of these, Li Ruzhen (1763-1830), protested against abuses towards women by including the issue in chapters of his satirical book, *Flowers in the Mirror*. In one of the chapters a merchant travels to the "Women's Kingdom" in which male and female roles are reversed. The merchant goes before the "King" of the land who is actually a woman. She asks him to go to a private apartment upstairs. There a series of surprising things happen to him:

"...In a little time, Merchant Lin was ushered to a room upstairs, where food of many kinds awaited him. As he ate, however, he heard a great deal of noise downstairs. Several palace 'maids' who were males ran upstairs soon, and calling him 'Your Highness,' kowtowed to him and congratulated him.

"Before he knew what was happening, Merchant Lin was being stripped completely bare by the maids and led to a perfumed bath. Against the powerful arms of these maids, he could scarcely struggle. Soon he found himself being annointed, perfumed, powdered and rouged, and dressed in a skirt. His big feet were bound up in strips of cloth and socks, and his hair was combed into an elaborate braid over his head and decorated with pins. These male 'maids' thrust bracelets on his arms and rings on his fingers, and put a headdress on his head. They tied a jade green sash around his waist and put an embroidered cape around his shoulders.

"Then they led him to a bed, and asked him to sit down.

"Merchant Lin thought that he must be drunk, or dreaming, and began to tremble. He asked the maids what was happening and was told that he had been chosen by the 'King' to be the Imperial Consort....

"Before he could utter a word, another group of maids, all tall and strong and wearing beards, came in. One was holding a threaded needle. 'We are ordered to pierce your ears,' he said, as the other four maids grabbed Lin by the arms and legs. The white-bearded one seized Lin's right ear, and after rubbing the lobe a little, drove the needle through it.

"'Ooh!' Merchant Lin screamed.

"The maid seized the other ear, and likewise drove the needle through it. As Lin screamed with pain, powdered

3. Lin Yutang, "Feminist Thought in Ancient China," *Tian Xia Monthly*, Vol. 1, No. 2 (Nanking, September, 1935), p. 130.

4. As quoted in, *Ibid.*, p. 144.

Manchu Emperor Guang Xi, who tried to outlaw footbinding   9

lead was smeared on his earlobes and a pair of 'eight-precious' earrings was hung from the holes.

"Having finished what they came to do, the maids retreated, and a black-bearded fellow came in with a bolt of white silk. Kneeling down before him, the fellow said, 'I am ordered to bind Your Highness's feet.'

"Two other maids seized Lin's feet as the black-bearded one sat down on a low stool, and began to rip the silk into ribbons. Seizing Lin's right foot, he set it upon his knee, sprinkled white powder between the toes and the grooves of the foot. He squeezed the toes tightly together, bent them down so that the whole foot was shaped like an arch, and took a length of white silk and bound it tightly around it twice. One of the others sewed the ribbon together in small stitches. Again the silk went around the foot, and again, it was sewn up.

"Merchant Lin felt as though his feet were burning, and wave after wave of pain rose to his heart. When he could stand it no longer, he let out his voice and began to cry. The 'maids' had hastily made a pair of soft-soled red shoes, and these they put on both his feet.

"'Please, kind brothers, go and tell Her Majesty that I'm a married man,' Lin begged. 'How can I become her Consort? As for my feet, please liberate them. They have...freedom.... How can you bind them? Please tell your 'King' to let me go. I shall be grateful, and my wife will be very grateful....'

"...a middle-aged 'maid' came up to him and said, 'Please, will you wash before you retire?'

"No sooner was this said than a succession of maids came in with candles, basins of water and spittoon, dressing table, boxes of ointment, face powder, towels, and silk handkerchiefs. Lin had to submit to the motions of washing in front of them all. But after he had washed his face, a maid wanted to put some cream on it.

"Merchant Lin stoutly refused.

"'But night time is the best time to treat the skin,' the white-bearded maid said. 'This powder has a lot of musk in it. It will make your skin fragrant, although I dare say it is fair enough already. If you use it regularly your skin will not only seem like white jade, but will give off a natural fragrance of its own. And the more fragrant it is, the fairer it will become, and the more lovely to behold, and the more lovable you will be. You'll see how good it is after you have used it regularly.'

"But Lin refused firmly, and the maids said, 'If you are so stubborn, we will have to report this, and let Matron deal with you tomorrow.'

"Then they left him alone. But Lin's feet hurt so much that he could not sleep a wink. He tore at the ribbons with all his might, and after a great struggle succeeded in tearing them off. He stretched out his ten toes again, and luxuriating in their exquisite freedom, finally fell asleep.

"The next morning, however, when the black-bearded maid discovered that he had torn off his foot-bandages, he immediately reported it to the 'King,' who ordered that Lin should be punished by receiving twenty strokes of the bamboo from the 'Matron.' Accordingly, a white-bearded 'Matron' came in with a stick of bamboo about eight feet long, and when the others had stripped him and held him down, raised the stick and began to strike Lin....

"Before five strokes had been delivered, Lin's tender skin was bleeding, and the Matron did not have the heart to go on. 'Look at her skin! Have you ever seen such white and tender and lovable skin?...'

"The footbinding maid came and asked Lin if he would behave from now on.

"'Yes, I'll behave,' Lin replied, and they stopped beating him. They wiped the blood from his wounds, and special ointment was sent by the 'King' and soup was given him to drink.

"Merchant Lin drank the soup, and fell on the bed for a rest. But the 'King' had given orders that his feet must be bound again, and that he should be taught to walk on them. So with one maid supporting him on each side, Merchant Lin was marched up and down the room all day on his bound feet. When he lay down to sleep that night, he could not close his eyes for the excruciating pain.

"But from now on, he was never left alone again. Maids took turns to sit with him. Merchant Lin knew that he was no longer in command of his destiny."[5]

Li Ruzhen hoped by his placing a male in the position of a concubine that this would point up the humiliation of this role for women. But it was not until the latter part of the 19th century that organized attempts were begun for reforms for women. Christians coming to China tried to end footbinding and started schools for young girls. At first, these missionary schools were looked upon with suspicion and few Chinese would trust their daughters to foreigners. The first Christian girls' schools were made up of girls bought by missionaries to raise or of girls from families so poor they could be bribed with food to attend school.[6] The communities were often very suspicious of these schools, particularly since Christians refused to accept or allow footbinding.[7] One rumor was that Christians were just buying up little girls to cut up and use for medicine![8] As time went on, however, these schools helped to change attitudes towards young girls.

Several anti-footbinding societies were founded, often with the joint cooperation of educated Chinese men and Christian missionaries or western business people in China. Kang Youwei was one of the male Chinese who organized an Anti-Footbinding Society in Kwangtung Province.[9] Mrs. Archibald Little, wife of a British merchant, began "The Natural Feet Society" in 1895. Mrs. Little described a meeting in Chongqing in which British and French women joined with Chinese women of many different dialects in a confusing, but rousing meeting to end footbinding:

"...There was a drawing-room meeting held at Chongqing in the far west of Sichaun; and it was a most brilliant affair. The wealth of embroideries on the occasion was a thing to remember....All the Chinese ladies laughed so gaily, and were so brilliant in their attire, that the few missionary ladies among them looked like sober moths caught in a flight of broidered butterflies. Every one came, and many brought friends; and all brought children, in their best clothes too, like the most beautiful dolls. At first, in the middle of the cakes and tea, the speeches seemed to bewilder the guests, who could not make out what they were meant to do, when their hostess actually stood up and addressed them through an interpreter. Then there was such eager desire to corroborate the statements: 'On the north bank of the river near Nanjing--' 'Yes, yes!' exclaimed a lady from Nanjing, 'they don't bind there! And they are strong-- very.' Then, when the speaker went on to say that on the road to Chengdu there was a city where a large part of the population

5. Li Ruzhen, *Flowers in the Mirror* (Berkeley: University of California Press, 1965), pp. 110–112.

6. Margaret Burton, *The Education of Women in China* (London: Fleming Revell, 1911), pp. 39–41.

7. The Catholic Church did accept girls with bound feet at first, but generally Protestant missionary schools did not.

8. Burton, p. 39.

9. Roxanne Witke, "Transformation of Attitudes Toward Women During the May Fourth Era of Modern China," Unpublished Doctoral Dissertation (Berkeley: University of California Press, 1970), p. 23.

19th Century Chinese women footbound but economically productive

all inter-married, and did not bind their women's feet, being of Guangzhouese descent, Guangzhouese ladies nodded and smiled.... And when the speaker further spoke of parts of Hunan where rich and poor alike did not bind, the two solitary representatives of Hubei, the boastful, could bear it no more, but with quiet dignity rose, and said, in their soft Hupeh voices, 'In Hubei, too, there are parts where no woman binds--none.' Next a missionary lady in fluent Chinese explained the circulation of the blood, and with an indiarubber pipe showed the effect of binding some part of it. There were no interruptions then. This seemed to the Chinese ladies practical, and it was quite striking to see how attentively they listened. This speech

was afterwards a good deal commented on. A Chinese lady then related how she had been led to unbind, ceasing any longer to feel delight in the little feet that had once been such a pride to her.... The meeting was then thrown open, and at once the very smartest of the Chinese ladies present came forward to make a speech in her turn. All present were agreed that footbinding was of no use, but it could only be given up by degrees. Man-man-de (Little-by-little) was the watchword. Then, just as at an English meeting, a number of ladies went on to a dinner party. But the others stayed and talked. 'Did you see my little girls listening?' said one mother. 'They are thinking they will never have their feet bound again.' And certainly the

Kang Youwei, philosopher who believed in women's equality

expression of the little girls had been eager in the extreme-- poor little crippled creatures! with their faces all rouged to simulate the roses of healthy exercise....

"At another footbinding meeting... when those opposed to binding were asked to stand up, all the men present but six rose to their feet, and a merchant among the audience began a speech against binding. Some days afterwards a mandarin, calling, took up Pastor Kranz's pamphlet lying on the table, and said: 'Ah, I have the larger copy of this book with pictures. No, I was not at the meeting the other day, but my people were. As to unbinding, the elder women can't; you see, their toes have dropped off. But my little girl of six is not having her feet bound any more. She screamed out so directly she laid her head upon her pillow, I could not bear to hear it. Besides, she got no sleep.' He was a man of means, and made no reference as to any possible difficulty about marrying her...."[10]

10. Mrs. Archibald Little, *Intimate China* (London: Hutchinson & Company, 1899), pp. 151-153.

Though footbinding seemed the most obvious abuse of women, its reform often made people look into other issues concerning women. In the last days of the Manchu Dynasty, for example, the Empress Dowager did suggest the creation of girls' schools. The 100 Days of reform of Emperor Guang Xu and Kang Youwei also stressed women's education and the end of concubinage. In the general reform movements in China (1890-1920, the 100 Days, the creation of the Republic and the May Fourth Movement), writers often mentioned women's rights as part of their programs. The following list suggests some of the male reformers for women in China of this era and the particular changes they stressed:[11]

Anti-footbinding:	Kang Youwei
	Gung Zizhen
	Liang QiChao
Anti-polygyny:	Zhou Zhian
	Chang Qing
Women's Political Equality:	Jin I
	Sun Yat-sen
	Mao Zedong
Anti-arranged Marriages:	Luo Jialun
	Chen Duxi
	Yang Chang-ji
Anti-forced Chastity:	Chen Qi-xiu
	Hu Shi
Women's Education:	Lan Dingyuan
	Xie Waliang
	Cai Yuanbei

These men -- along with Christian missionaries and a beginning group of educated Chinese women -- began the changes in Chinese attitudes toward women which would be one of the major reversals of traditional society. The next sections will suggest the changes, as reflected in the lives of individual women, were often painful, hard ones. But, at least, the changes had begun.

Points To Consider

1. What role might Christian foreign women have played in changing Chinese customs?

2. In the section from *Flowers in the Mirror*, what things does the merchant see de-humanizing which the Chinese might have seen as "natural" when done to women? What were some of the major issues concerning women which were stressed?

3. Why were so many of the early "feminists" of China male?

11. Witke, pp. 23-41.

14

B. The Fight for Education 1840-1930

If a woman were to go against traditional views of Chinese women, her first break with her family was likely to be about her education. This quarrel would often begin when she was six or seven and might continue until she was twenty. Sometimes the child would be defeated. An old working woman described how she was denied an education:

"...The foreign woman had a school for girls and urged my mother to send me to school. But my mother knew there was no use even to think of it.

My father became enraged at the very idea and would not listen. If I had been allowed to go to school how different my life would have been. I might have been somebody in the world."[1]

But sometimes, using a variety of weapons from temper tantrums to new family alliances, she would win. The chart below suggests how quickly education for girls became a growing ideal for China:[2]

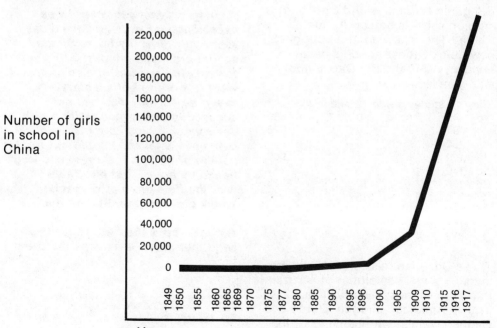

Number of girls in school in China

Year

1. Ida Pruitt, *A Daughter of Han* (Stanford: Stanford University Press, 1967), pp. 24–25.
2. Ida Belle Lewis, *The Education of Girls in China* (New York: Columbia University Press, 1919), p. 38.

15

The chart, which shows no girls' schools in China before 1840, is somewhat misleading. Girls in upper class families were often taught by private tutors so they did receive some education. Also, in certain parts of China, like Guangzhou, there seem to have been local neighborhood classes for girls taught by a mother or woman teacher.[3] But the idea of sending daughters "away to school" -- out of their neighborhoods and homes -- seems to have begun with the Christian mission schools.

The first schools for Chinese girls were in areas like Singapore, Malacca and Hong Kong where European traders had entries into these cities. The rest of China was closed to European trade until after 1840; then, with the merchant came the missionary teacher. In 1842, the first missionary school for girls was started by Miss Aldersey, a British woman, in the port city of Ningpo. Gradually, after 1864, girls' schools were allowed to go outside the delegated port cities and Christian mission schools spread throughout China.[4] The following chart suggests how quickly these schools became popular, using the Bei Dao school as an example:[5]

from	33 students with	2 teachers in 1888,
to	40 "	" 2 " " 1889,
to	91 "	" 4 " " 1899,
to	60 "	" 4 " " 1904,
to	120 "	" 7 " " 1909,
to	130 "	" 8 " " 1911,
to	180 "	" 10 " " 1913,
to	276 "	" 15 " " 1916,
to	409 "	" 24 " " 1918,
to	762 "	" 46 " " 1921,
to	879 "	" 51 " " 1923.

These Christian mission schools are, in many ways, something of a puzzle to fit into Chinese history. The British, American, French, Dutch and German women who came to China to teach were often in themselves breaking the stereotype of what the nineteenth century thought a homebody woman should be. Going off to China to teach was often as much an adventure, a break with tradition, for them as going to their schools was for their Chinese students. One missionary teacher, for example, wrote of the American male missionaries' prejudice against women teachers:

"...It is generally thought that the Chinese language is too difficult for the weak mind of a female.... There is now a lady in Singapore who speaks Chinese fluently. So I suppose, 'What woman has done, woman can do.'..."[6]

Not only did these teachers have to face language barriers, but they also had to struggle with money problems and the prejudices against girls being educated. Further, since most of these schools stressed Christianity, Chinese parents were reluctant to have their daughters exposed to what they saw as an "alien" religion. One missionary woman, Mrs. Baldwin, described the problems she had in opening a girls' school:

"During my first year here I was exceedingly anxious to have a day school for girls. My home Sunday school promised me over $70 a year towards the support of a school, so I went to work to get scholars-- everyone saying, 'You will not succeed in doing much with a girls' day school; others have tried and have always failed.' I could but try. I could not go into the street and visit house by house, but Mr. Baldwin, with the help of a native teacher, kindly did it for me. Still no one would promise to send the girls to school-- boys they would gladly send, but girls-- what was the use of

3. Mary Raleigh Anderson, *A Cycle in the Celestial Kingdom* (Mobile: Heiter-Starke Publishing, 1943), p. 51.
4. Roxanne Witke, p. 219.
5. Anderson, p. 109.
6. Henrietta Hall Schuck, as quoted in Anderson, p. 62. Mrs. Schuck did become quite proficient in Chinese.

School girls in the American Mission School at Weixian, Shandung, in the 1920's

teaching them? Mr. Baldwin came home feeling very much discouraged, as he had not secured a single scholar. Then I called the native teacher I expected to employ and told him that his having the place depended upon his getting enough scholars to open the school. He spent two or three days trying to induce parents of this ward to send their girls, but in vain. The usual stories were circulated as to what use we would make of the girls. The two most popular are-- we want to cut them open and make opium of them, and another, send them to Beijing and sell them to make medicine. Finally, the teacher said if I would give them a few "cash"[7] a day he thought I should succeed. Now this is the general custom, as the scholars usually do something at

home toward buying their rice; but I thought I would see if I could not succeed in getting them without this fee. I found there was no help so I said I would give them ten cash each day. I furnish books, pens, ink, etc., and yet must pay them to come and learn....

"The teacher, by the promise of the ten cash, had the promise of two scholars and I thought there would be no further trouble. I had the school room put in order, and the Saturday before the school was to open, purchased desks and put them into the room, locking them up. The first news that greeted me the next morning was that a thief had taken

7. cash-- in China it is a string of small coins strung together through a center hole worth a few pennies.

17

the lock off the school house gate, and carried off all my newly purchased furniture. All was replaced, but the two scholars did not appear. Still I was determined not to give up.

"There is an old man who has done considerable work for our mission.... I heard that he knew of two girls that wanted to be put in school, so I sent for him, and he came in a hurry, thinking we had some work for him to do. I said, 'Now, Ming Se, if you don't go right off and get me a sufficient number of girls to open my school and a teacher that the parents know and will trust, I will never give you any more work to do for me.' He laughed heartily and said he would go and get scholars and teacher, and in two hours he brought me two nice-looking girls and a teacher, and in less than another hour I had the third, and so the number increased from day to day until I now have in regular attendance from fifteen to seventeen girls."[8]

Despite these difficulties, the schools were expanded and became models for later government schools largely because they did seem to fill a need in China. The education given girls was important for their later lives, but sometimes the models presented by the Christian teachers was even more important. For example, one Chinese girl described how she felt about her Christian teachers after being tutored at home by her brother's male tutors:

"Until this time I had never seen any but men teachers. Indeed, it had never occurred to me that a teacher could be anything but a man, for the same word, xian-sheng, means both 'mister' and 'teacher.' But here most of my teachers were young women. And they were Chinese and not foreign. I looked on them with amazement and admiration, and followed their every move. How well they seemed to know their subjects.

"How self-assured they were. What dignity and authority they possessed.

Just as much as my old teacher. And then the light dawned. Their status was just the same as if they had been men. Here was real equality. This was what I had been feeling the lack of, without quite being able to put it into words for myself. This was the meaning of my growing feeling of injustice over the disabilities imposed by family and clan because I was a girl. I decided then and there that I would be like them....

"This was a feminine world. So was the women's part of our home in which I had grown up. But this Christian school was different. Women had a status here in their own right, and not by virtue of being the mother or wife of some man, and in danger of losing it in case of the death of the man on whom it depended. Here women stood on their own feet...."[9]

Other ways in which Christian schools modeled behavior were in physical education and attitudes toward marriage. Because these schools often stressed the necessity for girls to be active by playing field hockey or other games, footbinding was generally forbidden. Though many parts of the curriculum might stress embroidery or homemaking skills, the image presented by the unbound feet of teachers and students was that of an active woman. In attitudes toward marriage, teachers also presented different models. Some of the teachers were wives of missionary preachers and their marriages of affectionate sharing of responsibilities became models for their students.

The role of these missionary schools is not much stressed by the Communists, but their impact on China was significant, especially for women. The Christian mission schools not only meant the first

8. Margaret Burton, *The Education of Women in China* (London: Fleming H. Revell, 1911), pp. 39–41.

9. Wong Suling and Earl Herbert Cressy, *Daughter of Confucius* (New York: Farrar, Straus and Young, 1952), p. 209.

Girls in modern Chinese elementary school

formal girls' schools in China, but also the first co-educational elementary schools, the first women's colleges and the first co-educational colleges. Later Chinese graduates of these schools might rebel against their "Christian, imperialistic nature," yet, ironically enough, the movements for change in China (as in the strikes against National Humiliation Day, the May Fourth and December 9th Demonstrations) often were begun by students in these very schools.[10]

These schools, and the Chinese supported schools which opened after 1900, did offer real change in Chinese attitudes toward women. But the question for many women still

remained, "How do I get to go to school?" For some young girls this was not a major battle. Some had fathers who were reformers and who wanted their daughters to have excellent educations. For example, Princess der Ling and her sister and the Song sisters (Mei Ling, Eling, Qinling) were sent to Europe and the United States to study. But often a girl's education meant a family battle.

The beginning of the battle was when the girl got a bit of education

10. For example, several of the Chinese communist diplomats who met with Americans in China in 1972 had spent their student years at Christian colleges. See: John Israel and Donald Klein, *Rebels and Bureaucrats, China's December 9ers* (Berkeley: University of California Press, 1976).

and then was suddenly stopped. Zhou Zhongzhen described, for example, how a tutor was brought to their home to give English lessons to her brothers. She and her sister were allowed to share the learning. But when the brother went away to school, the tutor stopped coming. Though she and her sister were still eager to learn more, the family thought, "It wasn't necessary for girls to learn anything properly."[11] This stopping of education often led to a family confrontation.

It would seem that the parents would have all the advantages in the fight which followed. They controlled the money, they had physical force and they had the power of tradition behind them. When one Mongol girl wanted to go on to school, her father became violently angry:

"Timidly I approached Father and told him the schooling that I wanted. 'I don't want to marry,' my words rushed out, 'I want to come back to China and get a job and--'

"Father was glowering. 'Enough.'

"'But, Father--'

"'No more of this.'

"I had had all the education I was going to get. That was all there was to it.

"Later I listened to Father tell Mother: 'What's the use of Daughter learning a lot of drivel? You know as well as I that a girl can't support herself. Daughter couldn't earn a copper.' His voice was rising. 'Besides, it would give me a terribly bad name.'

"I was angry, so angry that I lost some of my fear of him and strode to his desk. 'I want to be a lawyer, Father. Or maybe a doctor.'

"'A woman lawyer! Hah, hah, hah!'

"In my anger I became very brave. 'When you marry me off, you will have to spend a great deal of money-- your position demands it. Please give me that money now for

my study? I promise that you won't have to spend anything for a marriage.'

"Father rose, towering, thickset as a gorilla. A heavy fist pounded the desk, a huge hand brushed everything onto the floor. 'Shameless!' His face was red, his eyes were popping. 'To pay for marriage, yes-- the sooner the better-- but'-- his fist rocked the desk-- 'for this imbecility, nothing!'

"The fist seemed to be crushing me and the eyes drilling into me. I fainted."[12]

In the face of such opposition, what weapons did the young woman have? The ultimate weapon was, for some, the threat of suicide. Xie Bingying described how she turned to the idea of suicide when her mother refused to let her go on to school:

"...I lost all hope of continuing school. When I realized this my heart was broken and I decided to commit suicide....

"In our village, all the ways I knew of committing suicide were:
  1. Hanging by a rope.
  2. Jumping into the river.
  3. Swallowing matches.
  4. Eating opium.
  5. Swallowing a ring.
  6. Cutting my throat with a knife.

"I was after all only a child; I wanted to commit suicide, but I was afraid of pain. I realize now that it was quite funny! Every day I debated with myself as to the best way of suicide....

"At last I decided to starve myself to death in bed.

"I stayed two whole days in bed, and everyone thought I was sick. Mother immediately called the nearsighted teacher who was also a doctor. 'She is not sick,' he said.

11. Zhou Zhongzhen, *The Lotus Pool* (N.Y.: Appleton–Century-Crofts, 1961), p. 103.

12. Liang Yan, *Daughter of the Khans* (N.Y.: W.W. Norton, 1955), pp. 52-53.

20

"My sister came to my bed and tried to comfort me. She wept with me....

"'Good Sister,' she said, 'tell me if there is anything you wish that I can do.'

"'No one can do it!' I said.

"'Tell me what is the matter,' she persisted.

"'I want... I want to study,' I said at last.

"Mother seemed to know that I was fasting because I wanted to study, and purposely paid no attention to me, which made me all the more determined to die. 'Mother loves her children so much, and yet why does she still refuse to consent when I am about to die?' I said, and I doubted her love.

"But on the third day, when she saw I was so stubborn, Mother consented. She said that for two years she was going to watch my behavior. If I improved after those two years, then I could go to school. If not, she would marry me off.

"Through this ray of hope my small life was saved."[13]

The problem with threatening suicide, of course, was that some families really might rather see their daughters dead than in foreign schools. There were some women who did kill themselves when denied an education.[14]

For other young girls, the way to get an education was to leave home. This was a desperate move as they often had little money and no respectable girl would be separated from her family. Two who did escape and have written about it claim it was only possible with the aid of friends or teachers.[15] In the case of Zhou Zhongzhen her escape to go to the university and to live at a Young Women's Christian Association hotel became a newspaper sensation. Her father promised to let her go to school if she returned, but she did not know whether or not to trust him. They then carried on their dispute by writing to a newspaper. Being a scholarly family, both her mother and father wrote her poems to be published:[16]

Her father's poem:

"I pray to God, and ask the seer: how else should I have acted?
The seer tells me you will be back before the fifteenth.
Time passes, and suddenly it is the fifteenth,
But my flesh and blood has not returned to me."

Her mother's poem:

"I had just taken the measurements for your shoes;
I devoted myself tirelessly to your welfare;
How could I know that you would grow up so stubborn;
Or that your love of learning would be deeper than your love for me?"

Her parents' poems were met with one of her own:

"The icy wind pierces my thinly clad body;
In the night I light my lamp and cannot sleep.
But I will not be defeated by hardships,
Father and Mother! A daughter is as good as a son!"

Eventually, she did convince her family to let both her and her sister go to school.

But the struggle to get an education was not necessarily carried on by the girl alone. Often her two most valuable allies were her mother and/or her elder brother. For example, the writer Ding Ling's mother openly broke with her family

13. Xie Bingying, *Girl Rebel* (N.Y.: John Day, 1940), pp. 30–32.
14. Paul Reinsch, "The New Education in China," *Atlantic Monthly*, April, 1909, p. 520.
15. Zhou, pp. 141–148; Liang, pp. 60–68.
16. Zhou, p. 174.

and took her daughter away to be educated.[17] Another woman's mother ignored family tradition by sending her two daughters to an American grade school because, her daughter wrote:

"...for no other reason she wanted us to start life right by learning to stand up to and get above men in the American way. How she got the idea that American girls enjoyed the most privileged position of all, I never found out, but mother had always wanted us to be stronger and more self-reliant than other girls of our acquaintance, and naturally she sympathized with my desire to be independent. We had always known she was an exceptional Chinese mother.... With such a mother behind me, the battle was won without too much effort...."[18]

An older brother sometimes also was a help. Often the family sacrificed to send the oldest boy in the family to the best schools available. Since, in the early twentieth century, these

17. Helen Snow, *Women in Modern China* (Hague: Mouton & Co., 1967), pp. 198–199.
18. Tang Sheng, *The Long Way Home* (London: Hutchinson & Co., n.d.), p. 14.

Women's Banking Department, Beijing, 1920's

were usually Westernized schools, the young men came home to encourage their sisters to change also. In the autobiographies of several Chinese women, their older brothers' role in supporting their struggles is mentioned. The following example from Xie Bingying's book is typical:

"In the winter Mother received a letter from Elder Brother, and in it there were a few sentences concerning me: 'My sister Phoenix has quite rare ability, worthy of a good education. Next spring we should send her to Dadong Girls'School, and prepare for her to go to the Girls' Normal School in the future. Nowadays girls are beginning to go out, and there are schools all around. Our family was always one of scholars. I hope Mother will not object just because she is a girl." [19]

Thus, with determination and help, young Chinese women did begin to get an education. But even when they studied hard, they did find some discrimination against them. One Chinese woman studying in Japan found that Japanese students looked down upon her racially. [20] Another young woman found she was scorned when she did too well in a co-educational class:

"I shall always remember geography class, one morning after the first monthly exams. When the teacher, a kind, friendly man with a smile always hanging around the corners of his fat genial face, walked in, the students began to ask him the usual questions. Who had passed, who had failed in the exams?

"He always bore their impish conduct with more good humor than it deserved....

"The teacher said, 'I am not going to tell you who flunked, you unruly band of rascals, but I can tell you that at yesterday's meeting of the faculty, it was decided that this class tops the list for noise and naughtiness.

However, it has been decided that one of you here shall get honors for exams as well as for behavior.'

"That started a rain of questions. All the boys were eager to know who the student was. Awei [the other girl in the class] and I sat in the back row taking no part in the discussion. Thoroughly enjoying the sensation he had created, the teacher proceeded steadily with the lesson and ignored the questions that kept coming up. All he would say was: 'Someone is going to be proud, and the others are going to be mighty ashamed of themselves.'

"'I wish he would hurry up,' whispered Awei to me. 'I want to know who it is. I hope he is presentable, as I do not mind talking to him if he asks me. I would like an intelligent sweetheart.'

"From our place in the back row we could see the whole class and observe their tricks far better than the master at the front. There was a reason for our being put in the back. On the first few days we had been put right in front of the class, but the boys teased us. They not only poked fun at us, but prodded us with rulers in parts of our anatomy that are not meant to be prodded, so that the wise Dean decided that our backs had better be protected by a wall. Sitting where we did, we were not attacked with rulers when we were trying to answer questions and did not have to try to look cool and dignified when we sat down suddenly on a thumbtack that some wicked little devil-boy had put on our seats.

"I don't think Awei liked the back seat very much, but I did, for I could throw paper at the boys' ears by an elastic catapult, and they never suspected that it was I.

"At the end of that lesson, the teacher was packing away his books as if he

19. Xie, p. 28.
20. Buwei Yang Zhao, *Autobiography of a Chinese Woman* (New York: John Day Co., 1947), pp. 140–142.

Elementary students playing in modern Chinese co-educational schools

had forgotten his secret, so the boys began to yell, 'Now, Master... tell us who has honors.'

"'You want to know? You are so interested in higher education?' the teacher queried. 'I am surprised. Well, I'll tell you: some have honors for work, of course, but the one who has honors for both behavior and the examinations is a girl, Guo Jinqiu.'

"There was dead silence. The teacher told me to stand up. I couldn't. Awei dug me in the ribs, and I got up, blushing. I had never meant to be as good as all that. If the faculty liked me that much, the other students would hate me. They would be jealous.

"'There she is, you little rascals,' said the teacher. 'Just a little girl, and she has beaten you all. Guo Jinqiu, I congratulate you.'

"I stammered and sat down-- on a thumbtack that some heartless boy had put on my seat. I squealed, and the whole class roared with laughter. I wept from sheer nerves. A message fell on my desk. I opened it. Some one had written my new name on it: Maiga, the school slang for bookworm. Before that, they had called me Garbo-- because I was tall, slim and seemed to want to be alone with my books. Now I was the bookworm."[21]

21. Helen Guo, *I've Come a Long Way* (New York: Appleton–Century, 1942), pp. 61–63.

With determination a young woman might finally succeed. One who did so describes how her wealthy father reacted to her success:

"...He spoiled me as he had never spoiled me before. He gave me all the good things to eat I had missed abroad. He had more than forty new Chinese dresses made for me.... He asked me what branch of medicine I was going to specialize in and where I would like to have my hospital set up. He would make preparations, so that it would be ready for me when I returned again. He arranged parties for me and introduced me to everybody as 'my daughter, Dr. Yang Buwei.'

"'You know,' he told his guests, as he drank to their health, 'I would rather have one daughter than ten sons....'"[22]

But even after these women had received an education, what then? They still had to face major issues yet to come -- marriage, career choices, and their roles as citizens. Education gave them strengths to face these new battles, but it was only the first round in a long fight.

Points To Consider

1. In what ways were the Christian missionary schools important to changing ideas about women?

2. Women trying to receive an education have often in China and elsewhere been "put down." What are some of the tactics used, as described in the examples, to keep women from striving for excellence? Are these tactics still used?

3. Why do you think these women went to so much trouble to be educated?

4. How did these women differ in their kind of education from those educated women of ancient China?

22. Buwei Yang Zhao, *Autobiography*, p. 145.

C. Resistance to Marriage 1900-1930

If old China and the new Communist China have one thing in common, it is that both have assumed men and women should be married. Single men or single women are still considered unusual. A recent American traveler to China found that her decision to remain unmarried was considered something of a mystery to her Chinese interpreters.[1] Virtually all women who hold positions of power in China are married. However, in the early twentieth century, the whole institution of Chinese marriage was under attack.

Part of the resistance to marriage came from young men and women rebelling against arranged marriages. Mao Zedong, for example, left his family when they married him off to a woman he had never seen. But while pressures were great on young men to fulfill their filial duty and marry the family choice, pressures on women were even greater. For example, one woman was threatened with death by her uncle if she refused the marriage arranged since her birth.[2] Yet, at the same time, giving in to an arranged marriage might have a greater impact on a woman's life than a man's. To use Mao as an example again, he set aside his first wife -- all that was needed for divorce -- and later married Yang Gaihui who shared his revolutionary views. But a wife had to go to live with her husband's family and divorce for her was impossible. Marriage into an unsympathetic family might mean a virtual prison, or even death. A famous farewell letter written in 1900 by a wife in such circumstances described her plight:

"I am about to die today because my husband's parents, having found great fault with me for having unbound my feet, and declaring that I have been [wrong] have determined to put me to death. Maintaining that they will be severely censured by their relatives, once I enter a school and receive instruction, they have been trying hard to deprive me of life, in order, as they say, to stop beforehand all the troubles that I may cause. At first they intended to starve me, but now they compel me to commit suicide by taking poison. I do not fear death at all, but how can I part from my children who are so young? Indeed, there should be no sympathy for me, but the mere thought of the destruction of my ideals and of my young children, who will without doubt be compelled to live in the old way, makes my heart almost break."[3]

While this woman was forced into suicide, other women chose suicide as means of rebellion. One of the cultural differences between China and Western nations has been that while men seem to commit suicide more often than women in the West,

1. Nancy Slaughter, conversation with authors, April, 1979.
2. Buwei Yang Zhao, *Autobiography of a Chinese Woman* (New York: John Day Co., 1947), p. 80.
3. Quoted in Paul Reinsch, "The New Education of China," *Atlantic Monthly,* April, 1909, p. 520.

Painting of Yang Gaihui and Mao Zedong, idealized wife and husband revolutionary team

in China women more than men kill themselves.[4] The unhappy and powerless state of being a daughter-in-law often led women to despair and suicide. At times this seemed the only way to escape. But besides an escape, suicide was sometimes an act of revenge. Suicides were thought to be unlucky and their ghosts might haunt the households.

There were other motives for suicide. Some of the "ideal women" of China kept their chastity by committing suicide. Other women used suicide as a protest weapon. One woman wrote letters concerning her future suicide by saying that she would sacrifice her life unless money was given for a girls' school.[5]

Because other avenues of protest seemed closed to women, suicide by women had traditionally been a part of Chinese society. In the early part of the twentieth century, then, it is not surprising to find that some

women resisted marriage by committing suicide as their wedding day approached. One of these suicides was that of Zhao Wujie, who slit her throat in the bridal chair that was carrying her to her wedding on November 14, 1919.[6] This particular case came to the attention of Mao Zedong and others who verbally defended her action. Though he felt it would have been better for her to fight her family, Mao claimed she did not kill herself. Rather, her family had killed her:

4. Cultural information on suicide from: Margery Wolf, "Women and Suicide in China," in *Women in Chinese Society*, edited by M. Wolf and Roxanne Witke (Stanford: Stanford University Press, 1975), pp. 111–143.
5. Reinsch, p. 519. After her death, money did come in to the school.
6. Roxanne Witke, "Mao Zedong, Women and Suicide," in *Women in China*, edited by Marilyn Young (Ann Arbor: Michigan Papers in Chinese Studies, No. 15, 1973), pp. 7–33.

"A suicide is determined entirely by the environment. Was Miss Zhao's original intention to die? No, it was not. On the contrary, it was to live. Yet her final decision to die was forced by her environment. Miss Zhao's environment consisted in the following: one, Chinese society; two, the Zhao family of Nanyang Street, Changsha; and three, the Wu family of Kantzuyuan, Changsha, the family of the man she did not want to marry. These three factors formed three iron cables which one can imagine as a sort of three-cornered cage. Once confined by these three iron cables, no matter how she tried, there was no way in which she could stay alive. The opposite of life is death, and so Miss Zhao died.... If one of these factors had not been an iron cable, or if she had been set free from the cables, then Miss Zhao would not have died."[7]

As Mao and many other writers, male and female, protested against arranged marriages, women began to follow other routes than suicide. One way some thought to avoid arranged marriages was simply to avoid marriage altogether. At various universities, for example, students took vows never to marry. Mao and his friends had so pledged, but later changed their minds.[8] Some women tried "free love," living with men without marriage. In a society which still prized chastity, and in which respectable jobs for women were hard to find, women who refused marriage found themselves in difficulties. For example, the writer Xiao Hong led what her biographer has called a rather "seamy" life, clinging to men who no longer loved

7. As quoted in Witke, p. 16.
8. *Ibid.*, p. 10.

People from the Revolutionary Generation

her and on whom she had no legal claims. In one of her books she described the clay idols of women, perhaps describing herself:

"...And why have the makers of idols cast the female figures with such appearances? That is in order to tell everyone that gentleness indicates a trusting nature, and that the trusting are easily taken advantage of; they are telling everyone to hurry and take advantage of them.

"If someone is trusting, not only do members of the opposite sex take advantage of them, but even members of the same sex show no compassion...."[9]

However, other women, like Ding Ling, seem to have followed some "free love" ideas with independence and strength.

But if a woman did not wish to risk losing her "respectability," nor did she wish to risk marriage, there was still another choice. She might be a single woman who refused to have any sexual relations with men. The woman who did not marry was not unknown in Chinese society. In the area around Guangzhou in the 19th and early 20th century, for example, there was a tradition of some women choosing not to marry. These women generally supported themselves by silk raising and had their own customs. They combed their hair in special fashion to show their determination not to marry; they had their own secret society and their own houses.[10] Though economic decline in the silk industry and the Communist government have mostly ended the tradition, traces of it still exist in areas like Singapore, to which Chinese single women have immigrated.[11]

In the first half of the century, women outside the area of Guangzhou also considered non-marriage. One traditional Chinese mother wrote letters to her family describing how terrible it was to think her daughter might remain unmarried and become a doctor:

"Canst thou imagine it? A daughter of the house of Liu a doctor! Where has she received these ideas except in this foreign school that teaches the equality of the sexes to such an extent that our daughters want to compete with men in their professions! I am not so much of the past as my daughter seems to think; for I believe, within certain bounds, in the social freedom of our women; but why commercial freedom? For centuries untold, men have been able to support their wives; why enter the marketplaces? Is it not enough that they take care of the home, that they train the children and fulfill the duties of the life in which the Gods place women? My daughter is not ugly, she is most beautiful; yet she says she will not marry.... I also quoted her what I told Zhibei [her brother], many months ago, when he refused to marry the wife thou hadst chosen for him: 'Man attains not by himself, nor woman by herself, but like the one-winged birds of the ancient legend, they must rise together.'

"My daughter tossed her head and answered me that those were doubtless words of great wisdom, but they were written by a man long dead, and it did not affect her ideas upon the subject of her marriage.

"We dare not insist, for we find, to our horror, that she has joined a band of girls who have made a vow, writing it with their blood, that, rather than become wives to husbands not of their own choice, they will cross

9. Quoted in Howard Goldblatt, *Xiao Hong* (Boston: Twayne Publishing, 1976), p. 120.
10. Marjorie Topley, "Marriage Resistance in Rural Kwantang," in *Studies in Chinese Society* edited by Arthur Wolf (Stanford: Stanford University Press, 1978), p. 247-269.
11. Marjorie Topley, "Immigrant Chinese Female Servants and Their Hostels in Singapore," *Man*, 1959, p. 213-215.

the River of Death. Fifteen girls, all friends of my daughter, and all of whom have been studying the new education for women, have joined this sisterhood; and we, their mothers are in despair. What can we do? Shall we insist that they return to the old regime and learn nothing but embroidery? Why can they not take what is best for an Eastern woman from the learning of the West, as the bee selects honey from each flower, and leave the rest? It takes centuries of training to change the habits and thoughts of a nation. It cannot be done at once; our girls have not the foundation on which to build...."[12]

Of course, some of these fifteen women may have later married, but some might not. Not to have children, especially when birth control methods were not entirely reliable, meant essentially a decision not to marry. Ye Chun and Lin Qiaozhi, both doctors currently important in China, are examples of Chinese women who chose careers over marriage.

But for the majority of the young educated women in China in the early 20th century, the resistance to marriage was only for arranged marriages. They hoped for a "new" style marriage, but resisted the old. They held out, like Song Meiling did, when her family disapproved of Chiang Kai-shek, until the family gave into her choice. Or they wrote to their unseen fiances telling them to cool off their interest. One woman described the letter she wrote and its results:

"So I wrote my fiance... a letter which stated in effect: 'Why don't you marry some one more to your taste? I intend to go to America or Europe to finish my studies and this does not seem to fit into your picture of marriage.' Then I put in some conciliatory phrases, suggesting that he marry some young girl, 'beautiful and worthy of bearing your name,

who will be a help to you in your devotion to your duty.'

"The hubbub which ensued was unbelievable. To the best of my knowledge no Chinese girl of good family had ever done such a thing before. Both families, especially mine, lost an enormous amount of face. My father was shocked beyond words, and, needless to say, my grandmother took to her bed and gave every appearance of dying of shock. My only support was Mother, who, though miserable at the disgrace which had been brought on the family, was still secretly happy that I had not been forced into the marriage. She cried a great deal, but she cried more from affection for me and general emotion than because of the end of the engagement. I had won the battle at a terrific emotional cost to the whole family."[13]

Another method of confronting an arranged marriage was to throw temper tantrums -- which may have been good psychological therapy considering the amount of anger one young woman said she felt:

"I was happily set for my adventure in Shanghai [to go to school] when sister Lucy broke the news to me that a marriage broker had got her eye on me and that I was going to be married to some wealthy young man.

"I banished myself to my room with my new suitcases, determined to do battle with tooth and claw to hold the little fortress of independence I had gained. I cannot describe the mood I was in. It was more than defiance; it was black, torturing anger. I decided I would kill myself rather than submit. Then I laughed at myself. I would kill the marriage broker and the wealthy young man. I would tear his face to

12. Elizabeth Cooper, *My Lady of the Chinese Courtyard* (Edinburgh: T. N. Foulis, 1920), p. 25-26.

13. Madame Wei Daoming, *My Revolutionary Years* (New York: Charles Scribner's Sons, 1943), pp. 26-27.

ribbons. I would kick him, beat him, and a lot more. So all my education was to be wasted; all my efforts had been for nothing! Why, I might just as well have lain down and been a pampered home-girl instead of adventuring on my own. I was just a piece of flesh. I was going to have to live with some man I didn't know. Why hadn't I been like Ahwei and had some romance? This was a trick. Brother had betrayed me. I barricaded myself in my room. If I was flesh, I would be hard flesh. I would never surrender.

"Then the black mood passed. I became logical as if by magic. No one could make me do what I did not want. I had learned that already. My mind would jump me over my difficulties like a flying horse. I kicked down the barricade of books and came out to meet the danger...." [14]

With determination and the support of some family members, resistance to arranged marriages was possible. Women then found their husbands at school or through mutual interest groups. When they did marry, they expected the husband and wife to be the affectionate center of the nuclear household. They expected no mother-in-law to come between them. Reforms of the Guomindang era also seemed to make for more modern marriages. "Mass" weddings were held so that several couples could marry simply and not burden families with the usual heavy wedding expenses. The 1931 Civil Code outlawed arranged marriages and official concubinage. Though this code was not much enforced in rural areas, it presented an alternative model for most educated Chinese.

These new laws, and the ones later revised by the Communists, did not create equality in marriage, but they did offer more choice for a woman and man in marriage. The question then became not the resistance to marriage, but reforms to be made concerning marriage. The "Refuse to Marry" tradition of Guangdang seems to have disappeared, Ding Ling was purged in 1957 for her "immorality" in supporting free love, and the unmarried woman in China is seen as an oddity now. One historian has suggested that Western and Chinese attitudes toward the family have been going in different directions. While the Western nations have been undergoing a questioning of various life styles for men and women, the Communists have not. They no longer ask the 1920's question of whether to marry. The emphasis is on everyone marrying.

Points To Consider

1. Why was the era of the 1920's open to different life styles concerning marriage? Why might these life styles be no longer popular in China?

2. Several tactics of avoiding arranged marriages were described. What other tactics might you also have expected people to use?

3. The writer, Pearl Buck, in one of her essays, criticizes men like Mao Zedong and Chiang Kai-shek for setting aside their first wives to marry more educated, companionable women. The divorced women often could not remarry and sometimes had no place really to go. [Pearl Buck, "Chinese Women," *Pacific Affairs*, October, 1931, P. 905-909]. Her suggestion was that these marriages should not be dissolved. The husband should continue his responsibility to her. Educated women should avoid marrying such men, as career women can take care of themselves, but the old fashioned wives cannot. Would you agree with Pearl Buck's answer to the dilemma posed by these arranged marriages?

14. Helen Kuo, pp. 67–68.

D. Women's Political Resistance 1900-1930

Having fought with their families to be educated and to decide for themselves about marriage, some women then turned to politics. Society had created the rules which limited women and by using the political process to change these rules, Chinese society would become more equal. For some women, their major focus was on working for change in women's rights. Other women emphasized anti-foreign movements and China's independence. Still others wanted a complete overhaul of Chinese society to make it a socialist state. These three groups all believed in equality for women, but they differed in the means by which to achieve it.

The women's rights movement in China was concerned with a variety of causes; educational opportunity, reform of marriage laws, and with the rights to vote and to work. By the early twentieth century, women's magazines and newspapers were suggesting new images for women. Bobbed hair and short skirts became the style in the 1920's. Women began to move into new economic roles; for example, they formed a special women's section of a Beijing bank.[1] But legislation to gain political rights came slowly. Though women had been in revolutionary armies and had participated in demonstrations to bring down the Manchu government,[2] the 1912 Constitution of the Republic gave men, but not women, the right to vote.

A Woman's Suffrage Alliance was created in 1912 and female demonstrators smashed the windows and stormed into the Legislature.[3] However, these rebellions did not receive organized support throughout the country. The dictator Yuan Shikai who then took power, was opposed to women's rights and the issue of voting was dropped until the 1920's.

In the 1920's various organizations, like the Women's Suffrage Association of Beijing, the Shanghai Women's Club and the Y.W.C.A. formed a Women's Rights League asking for the following:

"1. The opening of all educational institutions in the country to women. 2. Adoption of universal suffrage and the granting to women of all constitutional rights and privileges given to men.

1. Grace Thompson Seton, *Chinese Lanterns* (New York: Dodd, Mead & Co., 1924), p. 204.
2. Mary Rankin, "Elite Reformism and the Chinese Women's Movement: Evidence from the Kiangsu and Chekiang Railway Demonstration, 1907," *Ching-shih wen-ti*, Vol. III, No. 2, December, 1974, pp. 29–42.
3. Roxanne Witke, "Transformation of Attitudes Towards Women...," p. 70.

3. Revision in accordance with the principle of equality of those provisions in the Chinese Civil Code pertaining to relations between husband and wife, and mother and son, and to property rights....
4. The drafting of regulations giving equal rights to women in matters of marriage.
5. Prohibiting of licensed prostitution, girl slavery and footbinding.
6. Addition of a new provision to the Criminal Code to the effect that anyone who keeps a concubine shall be considered guilty of bigamy.
7. Enactment of a law governing the protection of female labor in accordance with the principles of 'Equal work, equal pay' and 'A woman is entitled to full pay during the time that she is unable to work owing to childbirth.' "[4]

For awhile in the 1920's some reforms for women were made, and women's sections of the Guomindang went to the countryside to explain the new marriage laws and educational opportunities. But these women became particular targets for attack during Chiang Kai-shek's takeover of power. Whether or not these women were Communists, "bobbed hair" was enough to count them as such. One newspaper reported that the most common form of punishment in Canton was to wrap these bobbed-haired women in cotton padded blankets soaked in gasoline and then burn them alive.[5] Punishments elsewhere were equally brutal.

During Chiang Kai-shek's term of power, some reforms were continued for women, primarily dealing with health and working conditions. But the 1936 Constitution did not include the right for women to vote. National suffrage for women had to wait until the 1940's. The women's rights movement in China was limited by the relatively few educated women in China, by foreign invasions and civil wars that disrupted peaceful political reform, and by the lack of Chiang's government's interest in women's issues.

Nationalism

Some women felt that women's rights were all connected with the desire for China to become an independent democratic nation. When this occurred, women would be recognized as first class citizens. Therefore, the main emphasis should be on liberating China. And there was much in the early 20th century to liberate China from. There were:

1) The Manchus -- imperial emperors of China

2) The Japanese -- their encroachments into China caused events like the National Humiliation Day in 1908 or the December 9, 1935, Protests

3) The Western Powers -- they gave Chinese territory away in the Versailles Treaty leading to the May Fourth, 1919, Protests

4) The War Lords -- they cut up China into pieces for their own use

Since these groups all had political and military power, change could only occur through demonstrations and/or violence. Perhaps the best known of the women who acted for nationalistic change for China was Qiu Jin 1875-1907.

Qiu Jin seems to have seen herself in the "women warrior" tradition of history. One of her poems described how she wished women to be:

4. Elisabeth Croll, *Feminism and Socialism in China* (London: Routledge and Kegan Paul, 1978), p. 98.
5. *Ibid.*, p. 157.

"Women's Rights"

"We want our emancipation!
For our liberty we'll drink a cup,
Men and women are born equal,
Why should we let men hold sway?

We will rise and save ourselves,
Ridding the nation of all her shame.
In the steps of Joan of Arc,
With our own hands will we regain
our land."[6]

But she also became very much involved in the fight against the Manchu government. She received some education in Japan, later broke away from her husband, but received some sympathy from her mother for her revolutionary activities. She helped to organize secret groups to propagandize and collect weapons to be used against the Manchus. As a school principal she helped to organize her Datong School to join others in an uprising against the government. However, informers gave Qiu Jin away and troops were sent to the school. She and some of her students resisted for awhile, but after two were killed and others wounded, she was captured.

Accusing her of treason, the local officials had her tortured and condemned to death and Qiu Jin was beheaded on July 15, 1907. However, her poems were published and she came to be considered a martyr to Chinese nationalism. Other women in joining the "Dare to Die" Regiments later on, saw her as a model for rebellion against the enemies of China. One of her last poems was particularly well-known because it combined the themes of her partiotism and her early death:

"The sun is setting with no road
ahead,
In vain I weep for loss of country.
Although I die yet I still live,
Through sacrifice I have fulfilled
my duty."[7]

Helen Snow, the American reporter, made the comment that "her [Qiu Jin] tomb in Hangzhou was the only woman's tomb in China to which the Chinese made pilgrimages."[8]

Socialism:

For women like Qiu Jin and other women who later would fight against the Japanese, the main issue was freeing China. But other groups of women believed that a complete change in society was needed. Some came to believe that through gradual, legal change, a better society could be made, and that there was no need for socialist government. Jing Youxia, for example, became the first Chinese woman judge and President of Shanghai Law School and worked on revision of marriage laws and other governmental reforms.[9] Another group of women became more radical in their beliefs and joined the Communist Party. The pattern for joining the Party was first an involvement in a protest that was put down by the government; for example, the May Fourth Demonstration, the Shanghai Textile Strike of the December 9th Demonstrations. Frustrations with seeing little progress towards reform possibly led women, as well as men, to become Communist Party members.

The woman the Communist Party in China stresses as most important in the era of the 1900-1930's was Xiang Jinyou. She became involved in politics as a result of the May Fourth movement in 1919. Because of her intelligence and organizing ability, she was chosen, along with Zhou Enlai and others, to go to France to

6. Quoted in Croll, pp. 68–69.
7. As quoted in Rankin, p. 1.
8. Helen Snow, *Women in Modern China* (Hague: Mouton & Co., 1967), p.99. However, Robert Payne says that in his recent trip to China, Qiu Jin's grave is virtually ignored. Why the Chinese Communists seem to ignore her is somewhat mysterious. Perhaps she takes away from Communist women heroes.
9. Jing Youxia, *My Revolutionary Years* (N.Y.: Charles Scribners Son, 1943), pp. 144–160.

Qiu Jin, revolutionary against the Manchu Government

learn more about socialism. When she came back, she joined the Communist Party and worked as a labor organizer in the Shanghai textile mills. Disturbed by the working conditions of women in these factories -- twelve hours a day and sometimes only board and room as wages -- Xiang tried to organize strikes.[10] These strikes were, for the most part, unsuccessful. She bitterly criticized not only factory owners, but women's rights groups. Xiang felt the emphasis on issues like women's suffrage ignored "deeper" economic issues.

This split between women who believed women's issues could not be solved by a generally male-led Communist Party and women who thought economic equality for women was impossible without class revolution was a major one.[11]

Because of her hard work and militancy, Xiang became the founder and first Chief of the Women's Department of the Chinese Communist Party. She also served in various other positions in the Party until 1928. She was then arrested in the "white terror" of Chiang Kai-shek. On May 1, 1928, she was executed and the books she had been writing were destroyed.[12]

After the "white terror," the Communist Party did gather some remnants of their party membership and tried -- at Hailufeng and Jiangxi -- to establish governments of their own and considerable reform for women was started. Eventually, however, the Communist Party went on the Long March to Yenan, but only 30-50 women went with them. Of those left behind some would survive; others like Mao's wife, Yan Kaihui, and his female cousin, Mao Zejian, would be killed by the Guomindang.

What was the role of these Chinese Communist women in the Party? Despite Xiang's emphasis on the overthrow of the whole society, most of the CCP (Chinese Communist Party) women seem to have been delegated to tasks dealing directly with women. They were not encouraged generally into power positions in other branches of the Party. The Communist reasoning for this was that the peasant women would be more able to talk to other women; speaking to "strange men" might get them into trouble. Therefore, the few educated women Communists were needed with the women's sections. Yet there seems to have been an ambivalence on the part of some of the male members of the Communist Party in accepting women in anything other than these women's sections. On one hand, as one male wrote, he really admired women who were "penalized doubly" (by being both female rebels and communists) and who bravely risked their lives.[13] On the other hand, the same Communist Party man wrote of his trying to live with an independent, spirited Chinese woman:

"Then I found that those very qualities of determination which made her a good revolutionary also made her stubborn and positive in her convictions. Once she had made up her mind....

"'You're worse than the party line,' I would say to her. 'You must be flexible and adjust to new conditions before being pushed into it.'

"But we were a two-man party, and no majority decision was possible. The vote was too often divided equally.

10. Suzette Leith, "Chinese Women in the Early Communist Movement" in *Women in China*, edited by Marilyn Young (Ann Arbor: Michigan University Papers, 1973), pp. 57-60.
11. The argument between a major emphasis on "feminism" or "socialism" continues today to separate women's rights advocates in Communist and Western countries.
12. Snow, pp. 248-249.
13. Nym Wales, *Song of Arian: A Korean Communist in the Chinese Revolution* (San Francisco: Ramparts Press, 1972), p. 325.

"I felt that I was being dominated... and this irritated me, for I was also of a positive, proud character.

"'Fortunately, we are not married, so she can't oppress me very far,' I would remind myself.

"'I never had much respect for my father's opinions,' I said once. 'But once he did say an intelligent thing. It was this: If a man's life is dominated by a woman, he is a slave 200 percent, If a woman is ruled by a man, she is only 50 percent a slave.'

"'We are exactly alike,' she would reply to all my criticisms. 'Everything you say to me I can also say to you.'

"She was certainly no burden to me. But to my surprise I found that I did not want her to be so free and competent. I felt that I was myself a burden on her good nature. In fact, I wished sometimes that she would get sick and appear helpless once in awhile so I could take care of her.

"'You know, I am out of my role,' I would say. 'I was born to fight for the weak and the oppressed. I am useless for such a competent person as you are.'"[14]

Thus, even a man committed to new values might have difficulty living with an independent woman. On the other hand, sometimes women did not feel completely accepted as equal members of the CCP.

Whether feminist, nationalist, Communist, or all three, the women political activists of early 20th century found the issues complex and their political activities often dangerous. The depth of their involvement, however, suggests how much they would risk rather than return to the past.

Points To Consider

1. Three types of women activists were described:

   a) those for women's rights first
   b) those for nationalism first
   c) those for the Communist Party first

   Why might it be difficult to combine all three commitments for a woman political activist? If you had been a young Chinese at that time, which of the three would have seemed to you to have the highest priority?

2. Of the seven reforms the Women's Rights League wanted in the 1920's, which are now outdated? Which might still be issues even in the U.S.?

3. Women activists were often "penalized doubly," according to some historians. In what ways might they be more noticed when trouble came?

4. The term "sexism" was not in use in the 1920's. But in what ways might the Communist Party then have been described as a "sexist" organization? What justification might the Party have had for placing women in the roles it did?

14. *Ibid.*, p. 241.

E. Chinese Women and the Arts: An Activity to Interpret Sources

Though Chinese women have participated in arts throughout China's history, some fields of art or literature have been closed to them during certain eras. The following sources give a brief glimpse of some of the ways in which Chinese women have used their artistic talents. In looking at these sources, decide whether or not the selection is from a *primary* or *secondary* source.

Primary Sources:
Eye witness accounts of people who actually were involved in or saw the events described in writing or pictures. Primary sources have the advantage of the observer having immediate contact with the event. However, their reporting may be distorted by limitations of their points of view.

Secondary Sources:
Interpretations of events by people who did not witness them. They may be by scholars -- such as historians -- who collect a great deal of source material about an event.

Evaluate each of the following fourteen sources as follows:

Check One

_____ Primary Source
_____ Secondary Source
_____ Not Sure

Write a short explanation of why you selected "primary," "secondary," or "not sure" for each source.

1. *"The recording of famous artists in dictionaries of painters was customary in China, though in many cases all we have are their names and a few words of praise. A curious discrepancy often occurs between facts in Chinese sources and their representation in foreign works; whereas Western books on Chinese art are almost exclusively devoted to male artists, leading one to suppose that women painters were extremely rare if not nonexistent, Chinese sources are abundant with references to women and often contain reproductions of their work. In fact, at the beginning of the nineteenth century, the art critic Tang Souyou wrote a remarkable book called* Yu-Tai-hua Shih *(Jade Studio Painting History) specifically about women artists and their contributions to the field."*
Source: Karen Petersen and J.J. Wilson, *Women Artists* (NY: Harper & Row, 1976), p. 160.

2. *As far back as 1964, Mao suggested that the story of the Red Lantern Society (the woman army during the Boxer Rebellion) be adapted for Peking opera. Due to interference*

and sabotage by the traitor, Jiang Qing, this directive of Chairman Mao's remained unexecuted. The China Peking Opera Troupe, working with revolutionary drive, produced the Red Lantern Society shortly after the downfall of the "gang of four," which was warmly acclaimed."
Source: *China Pictorial,* "The Red Lantern Society," March, 1978, p. 290.

3. *"Ma Chuan's (a Chinese artist) works are powerful, unusual. Her favorite themes flowers: the spear-orchid; the plum-blossom; the 'waterimmortal,' which we call narcissus; and a blossom called 'tea-flower.' The fame of Chuan was such that houses in the province which lacked a painting by the young woman were said to be without light."*
Source: Florence Ayscough, *Chinese Women Yesterday and Today* (Boston: Houghton Mifflin, 1937), p. 212.

4. *A picture in* Chinese Literature, *December, 1973, shows a painting by Ma YaLi. The title is "The Brigades Chicken Farm" and shows two women surrounded by chickens.*

5. *Ding Ling's insubordination (writing about women's rights), and certainly one reason for her tragedy (being arrested), lay perhaps in raising the right issues at the wrong time."*
Source: Yiqi Feuerwerker, "Ding Ling's 'When I Was in Sha Zhuan,'" *Signs,* Vol. 2, No. 1, p. 279.

6. *In the Qing (Manchu) Dynasty the ability of upper-class women to write poetry was esteemed enough to be accepted as part of a lady's dowry. A scholar-poet-official often preferred to marry an educated woman with whom he could have poetry contests, discuss the Confucian classics and the great poets. But in the same period the romantic notion that talented women were always ill-fated was a common one."*
Source: Kenneth Rexroth and Ling Zhang, *The Orchid Boat: Women Poets of China* (NY: McGraw-Hill, 1972), p. 143.

7. *Jiang Qing (Mao's widow) described her experience as a film actress to Roxanne Witke in her role as Nora in Ibsen's play, "The Doll House." "She had chosen to represent Nora as a woman rebel. In so doing, she went beyond Ibsen's original conception of the character, and in her judgment improved upon it. The audience clapped thunderously in response to her characterization. She added matter-of-factly that in those days it was rare for an audience to applaud any performer."*
Source: Roxanne Witke, *Comrade Jiang Qing* (Boston: Little Brown, 1977), p. 102.

8. *"In the eyes of many literary critics who have written about Xiao Hong, the excellence and importance of* The Field of Life and Death *have overshadowed everything she wrote subsequent to it; although many of her later works are treated favorably."*
Source: Howard Goldblatt, *Xiao Hong* (Boston: Twayne Publishers, 1976), p. 56.

9. *In the 1920's in the Chinese village of Ding Xian the folk plays called Yang Ke had a tradition in which "female parts were all played by men."*
Source: Sidney Gamble, *Ding Xian: A North China Rural Community* (Stanford: Stanford University Press, 1954), p. 17.

10. *A Chinese actress described how she got ready to act the part of the poet Cai Weng in the modern play "Cai Weng": "When I first took the role of Cai Weng in 1959, I felt a need to assimilate the spirit of a poet in order to bring this ancient heroine to life. I studied a great number of Chinese classical poems and concentrated on the comprehension and appreciation of the epic poem, 'The Eighteen Laments.' I did my best to penetrate right into the poet's*

innermost thoughts and feelings to gain an insight into her personal traits."

Source: ZhuLin, "I Played the Role of Cai Weng," *Women of China*, No. 2, 1979, p. 28.

Chapter 2

Diversity of Women's Lives Within China

Chapter Contents

A. Women of Tibet: A Variety of Life Styles

China, throughout its history, has been an area of diverse peoples. Though the Han Chinese have been the dominant group, there have been minority cultures which differed in customs and often contrasted to "traditional" values relating to women. The next three readings deal with the diversity of the people's of China, particularly focusing on minority women.

In 1951, after some token resistence, Tibet accepted the control of the People's Republic of China over its affairs of government. Since then there have been several unsuccessful revolts against the Tibetan Communist Autonomous Government set up by the Chinese in 1953. It is difficult to determine whether this Chinese Communist regime has generally helped or hurt the people of Tibet. A reform program has been started by the Chinese that includes land redistribution and abolition of the feudal class system. Roads have been built, medical care and schools improved and some light industries started. On the other hand, the Dalai Lama, who had led Tibet as Buddhist religious leader, and about twenty thousand other Tibetans have chosen to flee to exile in India rather than live under the Communists. Many Tibetans seem to object to the forcible takeover of their country by Communist China even though there have been some real benefits for many of them as a part of the People's Republic.

The Communists claim that they liberated the Tibetans from a dictatorial government. It did seem that Tibet's class system fit the belief of Chinese communism that the peasants were being suppressed by unproductive landlords who lived off the peasants' labor. For example, there does seem to have been a small group of wealthy nobles and a few religious monasteries that owned most of the land. They made heavy demands on the peasants that worked for them. These peasants seem to have been like medieval European serfs in that they were obligated to stay on the land of their masters whether it was that of a noble or a Buddhist monastery and they had to contribute crops and labor to these landlords. Some stories were told of cruel punishments of serf-peasants by the landlords. At the least, small groups of the nobles and some Buddhist monasteries were very wealthy while most Tibetans lived in poverty. As far as a severe class system is concerned, then, the Communist beliefs seemed to fit the situation in Tibet. Therefore, the Tibetan class system gave Communist China a possible reason to take over Tibet so as to bring about land reforms.

However, regarding women, the Communists found that their system of beliefs did not fit the situation in Tibet very neatly. By incorporating Tibet into their country, Red China gained control of an area that had a

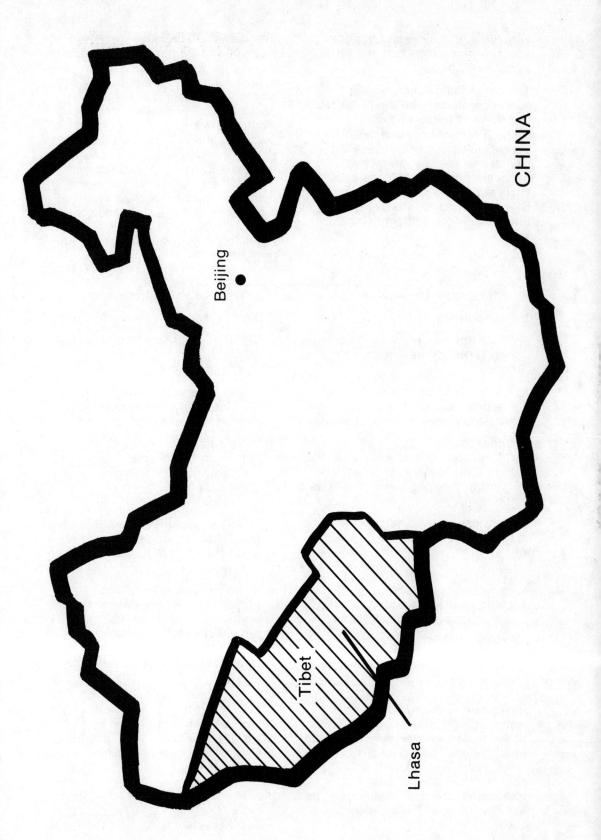

Beijing

CHINA

Tibet

Lhasa

43

very different history of attitudes toward women than had been true of traditional China.

The belief that women were a suppressed class like the peasants had seemed to fit pre-Communist China. From about the time of the Song Dynasty (c. 960-1279 A.D.) Chinese women generally had occupied positions of low status. A basic aim of the Communist Revolution was to improve dramatically the status of Chinese women.

Traditional China had suppressed women. The Communists saw this as a part of a general system of suppression -- the traditional Confucian system that kept the peasant in a low position kept women down as well. The incorporation of Tibet into the People's Republic of China created problems for the Communists with these beliefs. Although it appears that Tibet did have a class system that greatly benefited a small landlord group, its women traditionally enjoyed high status and open roles.

Traditional Chinese Women

1. Bound their feet

2. Could not own property from their own family or their husband's family

3. A wife could be cast off for seven reasons, but could not divorce her husband even if cruelly treated

4. Under the instructions of Confucius, were ruled by men from birth to death and had few economic responsibilities outside the home

5. Were expected to seclude themselves and stay at home

6. Only had one husband, but a man could take a concubine -- widows were expected not to remarry.

Traditional Tibetan Women

1. Did not bind their feet

2. Could inherit property

3. Could quite easily obtain divorces -- in fact, it was fairly common for women to divorce, but not for men

4. Were known for business and administrative talents -- very often taking over government or business positions for their husbands[1]

5. Were not secluded and although marriages were arranged, women knew their future husbands before marriage

6. Quite frequently practiced polyandry -- where one woman married several brothers -- or a type of polygyny where a family of sisters married one man who went to live at their home

---

The question of how this higher status of Tibetan women came about has not been satisfactorily answered by social scientists. The situation for women of Tibet is particularly surprising because of the traditionally low status of women in India and China, Tibet's neighbor cultures.

Tibet is a large country[2] situated on a high plateau surrounded by the Himalaya Mountains. Possibly Tibet's isolation from other cultures

1. Giuseppe Tucci, *Tibet: Land of Snows* (New York: Stein and Day, 1967), p. 155.
2. Tibet is six times the size of the British Isles or about twice the size of Texas.

A peasant woman from the herding area of Tibet

permitted its people to develop their own views of women. Tibet is not only isolated but its geographic position creates great difficulties for human habitation. Tibetans live in the highest country in the world which causes unique living conditions.[3] The hot sun pierces through the thin air and heat can be followed quickly by sudden and violent chilling cold winds. Most Tibetan peasants struggle to gain a living from infertile land while dealing with the additional problems caused by this very high altitude. Perhaps these difficulties forced peasant men and women to struggle together against nature -- so there developed a rough equality between them.

Women do have a prominent place in Tibet's history and religion. The first great king of Tibet, Songsten Gambo, married two princesses -- one from Nepal and one from China -- so as to help secure the borders of his newly united country. Both the Nepalese princess, Bhrikuli, and the Chinese princess, Wen Zheng, were Buddhists. Wen Zheng was especially important to Tibetan history.

In the year 652 A.D. she journeyed from her home in the ancient capital of China, Xian, to marry King

3. The average altitude of Tibet is 12,000 feet, but parts are as high as 16,000 feet. Some areas have a permanent frost on the ground while a small area in the south is damp and tropical.

Songsten Gambo in Lhasa, Tibet. According to a Tibetan legend, she brought with her as a wedding gift for her husband, the king, the most fabulous and holy religious object of Tibet -- the Altar of Jo. This priceless image of the Buddha is created of gold, silver and jewels and is kept in the Jokhan Temple in Lhasa. It was Princess Wen Zheng who was particularly influential in the conversion of King Songsten Gambo to Buddhism from the local Tibetan religion of Bon.

Other queens and also female deities have been important to Tibetan culture. For example, there were Palden Lhamo -- a fierce and terrifying female god who was the guardian of the Holy City of Lhasa, and also Mandarava, who according to legend, married the 8th century Tibetan saint, Lopon Rinpoche, against the wishes of the king, her father. The king had Mandarava and Lopon burned at the stake, but the fire turned to water and the stake into a lotus. They were saved. Also important was Dolma, wife of Chenresig, the protector deity of Tibet. Dolma was worshipped in her own right.

Female gods may have been especially prominent because Tibetan Buddhism was heavily influenced by the Indian Tantric cult. The Tantrics worshipped the "female principle" or creative part of the universe, in the form of woman and mother. Their female god, Shakti, was supreme. Around 1000 A.D., Tibetan Buddhism accepted many Tantric ideals. Women gods became important and even ordinary Tibetan women may have gained status because of the importance of women in the Tantric.[4]

Several observers have said that various marriage and inheritance customs have had a positive influence on the position of women in Tibet. Of particular interest to social scientists have been the customs of polyandry and "reverse" polygyny.

Tibetan polyandry (a woman marrying several men) usually seems to involve rather poor families of animal herders who can only raise a specific number of animals on the family's limited land. To avoid breaking up the family property, all the brothers marry one woman. In this way only one family continues to exist and the property is not divided.

It might seem that such an arrangement would lead to jealousy and arguments between brothers. However, two recent European travelers to Tibet observed several polyandrous marriages and suggested that they generally seemed quite happy. Both these reporters felt it was because:

"...Children are all regarded as those of the eldest son. In all cases that I investigated the arrangement seemed to work amicably. The eldest son has prior rights. He is the master. Generally one son, the youngest, would be a monk, one out with the herds, one hunting; someone has to go to fairs and so on. There would be few occasions on which they were at home together for long periods. Since the property remains in the family, the question of which children are of which father has no economic significance."[5]

All the children of a polyandrous marriage were attributed to the oldest brother as father. Sometimes a younger brother would decide he wanted a wife of his own. If he got permission from the family, he could marry another woman and include her in the family. However, he would still be married to the first wife -- so in this case there would exist both polyandry and polygyny! It seems

4. Thubten Norbu and Colin Turnbull, *Tibet* (New York: Simon and Schuster, 1968), pp. 153-168.
5. Alan Winnington, *Tibet: Record of a Journey* (London: Lawrence & Wishart, 1957), p. 100. See also: Giuseppe Tucci, *Tibet*, p. 159.

that polygyny has been more common in various cultures than has polyandry. Therefore, when the custom of polyandry exists, social scientists have been interested in the results of this custom. For example, there is the problem of population imbalance. Depending on the time in the past, from 1/5 to 1/10th of all adult Tibetan males were celibate monks who never married.[6] It has been roughly estimated that about 20 percent of all marriages were polyandrous.[7] Therefore, there must have been many "extra" women who could not find husbands. It would appear that monastic life of men and polyandry would hurt Tibetan women's status by causing population imbalance. Actually, polyandry may have helped to improve the status of women. There was an imbalance of more unmarried women than unattached men; however, it was not as extreme as it might have been:

--- Although there are not the reports of female infanticide by travelers, there was a high rate of women who died in childbirth.

--- Though not as many as male monks, there were women nuns who lived celibate lives and never married.

--- If a woman never married, she could inherit a share of the family property. Therefore, it was respectable to be a single woman in Tibet and she had property to live on.

--- Especially in wealthy families who had all daughters, sometimes parents married them all to one man and brought him to live at their home. In this way their family property would not be broken up. This is a sort of "reverse" polygyny in which the husband goes to the wife's home instead of the more usual situation where the wife moves to the husband's home.

--- Some wealthy men also took several wives (polygyny).

This variety of forms of marriage in Tibet probably helped to enhance women's status because it gave them a number of choices or options. It was respectable for a woman to marry or to remain single, to become a nun, the wife of several brothers or one of several wives to one man. A man who entered into any one of these marriage forms was not looked down upon.[8]

The existence of these choices was probably of great advantage to women in Tibet. Additionally, the fact that they could inherit property and that they could divorce their husbands gave Tibetan women more rights and freedom than women of traditional China.

It seems then, that Tibetan women's higher status might have come from several sources:

1) the isolation of Tibet from surrounding cultures where women had lower status

2) the harsh living conditions which perhaps demanded a rough equality

3) the important place women had in Tibetan history and religion

4) the influence of the Tantric cult on Tibetan Buddhism

5) marriage, inheritance and divorce customs that favored women

6. Celibate: One who remains unmarried and does not have sexual relations -- especially for religious reasons.
7. Prince Peter of Greece and Denmark, *A Study of Polyandry* (The Hague, Netherlands: Moulton and Company, 1963), p. 416.
8. There were occasional uxorilocal marriages in China where a man went to live at his wife's home because the family had no sons, but this husband was looked down on by the community.

Whatever the sources of this higher status, Tibetan women have presented the Chinese Communists with a problem of justifying their takeover of Tibet on the grounds of communist ideals. By their notions the severe class system of Tibet should also have meant a low status for women. However, in traditional Tibet women had enjoyed a high status -- much higher than in China. Though they might improve women's lives in the class system, it would be hard to reason that the Communists were going to liberate Tibetan women from sexual suppression when they already enjoyed freedom.

Points To Consider

1. What things about Tibetan culture might have influenced the comparatively high status of women there? Why might the fact that there are several respectable options concerning marriage raise women's status?

2. Polyandry[9] (a woman marrying more than one man) probably seems a very strange custom to us. Why may it seem more strange than polygyny (a man marrying more than one woman)? Why do you feel the custom of polyandry might have improved the status of women in Tibet? Why did these marriages seem to usually work out fairly well? One anthropologist says that modern young couples in Tibet object to marrying polyandrously. Why do you think this custom might die out?

3. Why do the Chinese Communists have some difficulty fitting Tibet into communist philosophy and, therefore, justifying their incorporation of Tibet into the People's Republic of China?

9. For a good discussion on the reasons for polyandry see: Prince Peter of Greece and Denmark, *Polyandry*, pp. 552-574.

B. The Norsu: Slave Women and Women as Slave Owners

In the inaccessible, rugged Xiao Liang Shan or Cool Mountains of Southwestern China live a tribal group called the Norsu.[1] Until recently little was known about them except that they were greatly feared by peoples of the nearby valleys. The Norsu were slavers who raided the surrounding villages to capture people whom they took back to the Cool Mountains as slaves. In 1957, after a long struggle, the Chinese Communist government finally was able to persuade the Norsu to give up slaving and to free their slaves. In 1956-57 Alan Winnington, an English reporter for the communist newspaper, *The Daily Worker*, traveled to the Cool Mountains to learn about these fierce tribal people. He found that their treatment of slave women was often shockingly rough and cruel. On the other hand, high class, noble Norsu women had an unusually high status in their own society. Winnington felt that in some ways they had a higher status than Norsu men. The following are two selections from Winnington's book on his travels. The first is the story of an escaped slave woman, Ashi Vugan.

The Story of Ashi Vugan:

"By 1956 the trickle of runaway slaves had become appreciably heavier. I had several interviews with women slaves who had run away at that time-- formerly women slaves never did this, preferring to commit suicide. Precisely because they did not try to escape, female slaves were more expensive than men.

"A talk with Ashi Vugan provided an insight into the feelings at the time she escaped-- June, 1956. She was, I would say, a typical house-slave, unbelievably lacking in knowledge. It took a long time to get her to answer very simple questions....

"Ashi Vugan had no clear idea of her background. At first she said she was a Han who had been abducted as a child, then corrected this to say that her parents had been abducted Hans and she herself was born in slavery. She had been sent to accompany her mistress to her husband's house. Her master, Bayu Tierz, owned thirty slaves.

"Like many slaves, she planted a tiny patch of opium to sell and buy clothes and a little extra food. Two of her fellow slaves died of starvation, another had died in the course of a ferocious flogging. Vugan herself had tried to commit suicide once by eating opium but succeeded only in making herself very ill, for which she had been hung by her wrists and whipped.

1. Another more common name for the Norsu was Lualos-- an insulting label given them by the Han Chinese.

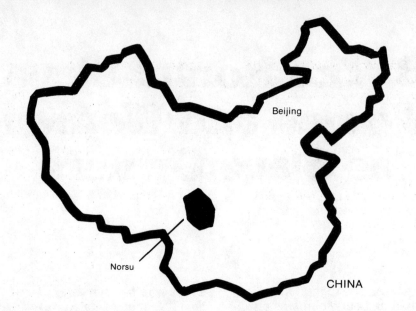

Beijing

Norsu

CHINA

"In June, 1956, she and another slave had been beaten almost to death. 'Blood came out of the other woman's mouth,' said Ashi Vugan. It was after this that the two girls-- Ashi Vugan was only a little over twenty-- discussed whether to run away to Ninglang, which was one day's walk away....

"As soon as the master and mistress were asleep a few nights later, the two girls had gone out, saying to the other slaves that one was going for firewood and the other to relieve herself. They fled, running as fast as possible for a long way and in the morning reached Ninglang.

"They went to a building which turned out to be the county government where they explained their plight. 'We were very scared,' said Ashi Vugan, 'because there were some people there who looked like [Norsu] nobles, looking at us all the time.' The clerk told them in a loud voice that they ought to return to their master and gave them each a big piece of corn bread.

"They left [sadly] not knowing what to do next and another clerk came out behind them. He passed them and said, 'Follow me.' They went with him into another building where he announced that he was a Communist. This man said it would be better if they left the Cool Mountains for a

time and arranged for them to go to Li Jiang to study. After a year learning to read the Han language and arithmetic, Ashi Vugan came back. Her district had already been reformed and she was free to take a job in the producer co-operative. Her old master, Bayu Tierz, was now working for the county government and by a twist of coincidence she took her meals in the same government-run canteen every day.

"'Are you friendly with him now?' I asked. For the only time during our talk she showed animation. Her eyes narrowed, and she said, 'We never talk to each other.'"[2]

This second excerpt shows the high status and power of noble Norsu women in contrast to their slave women:

"Norsu society preserves what appears to be strong traces of an earlier matriarchal[3] form.... Women occupy a high position in aristocratic Norsu society, some people even place it higher than that of men. I met one fiery little wine-bibbling warrior with a reputation for fierceness who admitted that if his wife told him: 'No drink today,' he would not take a

2. Alan Winnington, *The Slaves of The Cool Mountains* (London: Lawrence & Wishart, 1959), pp. 63-65.
3. Matriarchy is where the mother is head of the family and descent lines are traced through the mother.

drink. Moreover he would go home to his wife and specifically report: 'I have heeded your words and taken no drink.' I was told that if he failed to obey, it was quite on the cards that she would commit suicide and this would then become a clan matter, probably leading to war. Threat of suicide by Norsu wives is very common, and it is not an idle threat. Norsu women are extremely sensitive to what is regarded as a social affront or loss of face.... A case is cited which occurred in 1949, showing how heinous an insult it is for a stranger to touch the skirt of a Norsu woman. During the mediation of a feud, a wealthy commoner, trusting his own nobles to protect him, ostentatiously pretended to lift the skirt of a noble woman in order to annoy the other side. His own people rounded on him and he had to pay a fine of 4,000 ounces of silver to the enemy clan to save his own life.

"Norsu noblewomen's powerful position seems to derive from two prime sources. Clan protection is one; the other is their economic position. Women inherit their share of the main wealth of the Norsu society-- the slaves-- in their own right....

"Daughters inherit horses, cattle, sheep and silver equally with the sons and they also have other private property. While the males go around fighting and squandering their wealth, mothers save up for their girls from birth onwards. Slaves, horses, cattle, accumulated silver and heirlooms are taken by the betrothed to her husband's house and part of the enormous wedding gifts of the groom to the bride's family is given to the bride to carry back as her own to her husband's house. Since marriages mostly take place between families of approximately equal status a wife's property is generally greater than her husband's.

"Women have the determining voice in the household and a wife's

agreement must be sought in any important matter. In feuds, if the fighting becomes too fierce and general, the noblewomen on either side may come out and wave their skirts or cloaks. Fighting must then stop at once. It is a heavily sanctioned and grave social crime to kill a woman. Indeed it is generally held that women must not be attacked at all...."[4]

Points To Consider

1. What things bothered you the most about the treatment of the slave woman?
2. Why do you think the official loudly announced to Ashi Vugan and her friend to return to their master? Why might the Communists help these women to escape, but avoid doing it in a public way?
3. How did Ashi Vugan feel about her old master when she had to eat in the same canteen with him after she became a free person?
4. What specific things about Norsu society -- their laws and customs --made it possible for women to maintain power and high status?
5. In traditional China women often threatened or accomplished suicide to protest ill-treatment from their husbands or especially their mothers-in-law. The married Norsu women also use this weapon to win favorable treatment. In what way does their use of the threat of suicide seem different from that of traditional Han Chinese women? Why do you think the Norsu woman's threat was perhaps more effective in getting her way?
6. In Winnington's book he also describes several tribal groups such as the Jinpo and Wa in southwestern China where women have had higher status than the traditional Han Chinese women. Why do you think these women from small tribal minority groups might have higher status than women of the traditional Han Chinese majority?

4. Winnington, *Slaves*, pp. 42–44.

C. Women of the Manchus and Mongols — Part of the Ruling Elite

China, like most other large nations of the world, is made up of various ethnic groups.[1] Two of these ethnic groups had a particularly important relationship to the Chinese because the Mongols and the Manchus were peoples who had conquered China and ruled it.[2] While the Mongols and the Manchus did have different cultures and languages, they were similar to each other in some respects. For example, both were proud of their military heritages, both groups saw themselves as racially similar so that they approved of intermarrying and both cultures assumed somewhat more open roles for women than did the Han Chinese.

Since these cultures depended heavily on military expeditions, it is perhaps not surprising that Mongolian and Manchu women originally knew how to ride horses and often took part in polo games.[3] Mongolian women sometimes had their own military forces to command. While Mongol and Manchu cultures were still male-dominated, women seemed to move about freely and to have some choice in their marriage partners.[4] When these women moved into China, however, they found some clashes between their culture and the Han Chinese culture. Though many

1. June Teufel Dreyer, *China's Forty Millions* (Cambridge: Harvard University Press, 1976), p. 277-278. The major ethnic groups include:

Name	Population	Areas of Chief Distribution
Zhuang	7,780,000	Guangxi, Yunnan
Hui	3,930,000	Ningxia, Gansu
Uighurs	3,900,000	Xinjiang
Yi	3,260,000	Sichuan, Yunnan
Tibetans	2,770,000	Tibet, Sichuan, Qinghai
Miao	2,680,000	Guizhou, Hunan, Yunnan
Manchus	2,430,000	Liaoning, Kirin, Heilongjiang
Mongols	1,640,000	Inner Mongolia, Liaoning
Puyi	1,310,000	Guizhou
Koreans	1,250,000	Kirin
Tung	820,000	Guizhou
Yao	740,000	Guangxi, Guangdong
Pai	650,000	Yunnan
Tu-jia	600,000	Hunan, Hubei
Hani	540,000	Yunnan
Kazakh	530,000	Xinjiang, Qinghai
Tai	500,000	Yunnan
Li	390,000	Guangtong
Lisu	310,000	Yunnan
Wa	280,000	Yunnan
She	220,000	Fujian
Gaoshan	200,000	Taiwan
Lahu	180,000	Yunnan
Shui	160,000	Guizhou
Dongxiang	150,000	Gansu
Naxi	150,000	Yunnan
Jing po	100,000	Yunnan
Kirghiz	68,000	Xinjiang
Tu	63,000	Qinghai, Gansu
Daguors	50,000	Inner Mongolia, Heilong
Molas	44,000	Guangxi
Qiang	42,000	Sichuan
Bulang	41,000	Yunnan
Salars	31,000	Qinghai, Gansu
Maonan	24,000	Guangxi
Qilao (Kelao)	23,000	Guizhou
Xibo	21,000	Xinjiang
Tajiks	15,000	Xinjiang
Pu-mi	15,000	Yunnan
A-Chang	10,000	Yunnan
Nu	13,000	Yunnan
Uzbeks	11,000	Xinjiang
Russians	9,700	Xinjiang
Ewenke	7,200	Inner Mongolia
Penglong	6,300	Yunnan
Bao-an	5,500	Gansu
You-gu	4,600	Gansu
Jing	4,400	Guangdong
Tatars	4,300	Xinjiang
Menba	3,800	Tibet
Tulung	2,700	Yunnan
Elunchun	2,400	Inner Mongolia
Heche	600	Heilongjiang
Loyü	?	Tibet

Chinese customs became a part of their lives, some differences remained.

One of these differences was in appearance. All three groups — the Chinese, Mongolians and Manchus -- believed that they were racially superior to the other.

2. The Mongolian Dynasty, the Yuan Dynasty, lasted from approximately 1279-1368 A.D.; the Manchus, the Ch'ing Dynasty, ruled China from 1644-1912 A.D.
3. Princess der Ling, *Kowtow* (New York: Dodd, Mead & Co., 1929), p. 47.
4. Katharine A. Carl, *With the Empress Dowager of China* (New York: Century Company 1906), p. 223.

Mongol horsewomen in 1920's

Differences in appearance sometimes created problems, but these were generally solved by the non-mixing of the groups. The Mongols and Manchus might inter-marry with each other, but they did not, except in the lower classes, marry with the Chinese.[5] This separation even included women's visits to each other. The wife of an American ambassador to China around 1900, for example, found she had to give separate parties for Chinese and Manchu women.[6] The Manchus refused also to have any noble Chinese women at court; the empresses and concubines were all Manchu. But the Chinese also encouraged this separation. The following incident is from the autobiography of a Mongol woman telling of her experience in a Chinese school around 1920:

"The girls saw that I was different...: My nose was straighter than theirs and had more of bridge; my cheekbones were higher, and my hair, though dark, wasn't their jet-black. 'Gao Bize!' they shouted-- 'Straight Nose!' It was a common name among the flat-nosed Chinese for Tibetan lamas, Xinjiang traders and other outlanders of China who came into their midst. A Westerner was 'Big Nose' to them, for his nose usually is not only straight like an outlander's but even bigger. And my schoolmates jeered, 'Huang Mao!' (yellow hair) at me the way they jeered 'Red Hair!' at Westerners on the streets.

"Before long the girls learned from their parents why I looked different. 'Tartar!' they hooted. 'Barbarian!' In China, as perhaps in much of the world, another people is looked on with distrust, with hostility-- especially a people who once were China's conquerors."[7]

Besides emphasizing racial differences, the groups also had different emphasis on physical appearance and dress. Manchu court women, for example, had a special hair style -- sort of winged, butterfly fashion -- which only they wore. But perhaps the greatest difference between Mongols and Manchu women and the Chinese concerned footbinding. The tradition of more physical freedom for women among the Mongols and the Manchus may have been the reason for their opposition to footbinding. Though one of the Manchu emperors, Kang Xi, tried to end the practice of footbinding, the Manchus generally left the Chinese customs to the Chinese. Manchu women, like the Empress Dowager Ci Xi, were proud of their ability to move about and be more active than Chinese women. However, sometimes their facing a culture which emphasized small feet as the most erotic feature of a woman was difficult. For example, a Manchu woman described how she felt as a child when told she had "big feet." A neighbor's servant woman kept bringing the girl's feet up as a subject that would prevent a good Chinese marriage:

"There were those big feet again, when I was proud of the fact that my feet were small! I would assuredly talk this grave matter over with Father, ask him all about big feet, and why Manchus were believed by the Chinese to be such impossible people-- their girls unfit for marriage to Chinese!

"Somehow I managed to contain myself in patience until I could catch the ear of my father. I waited with fair patience, for I wanted much of his time, wherein to ask him about marriage, brides, Manchus, and big feet, but it seemed like an age before

5. The Manchus never conquered the Mongolians, but had formed an alliance with them against the Chinese. Therefore, both groups regarded each other as conquerors of China. Owen Lattimore, *The Mongols of Manchuria* (London: George Allen, 1934), pp. 60-61.
6. Sarah Pike Conger, *Letters from China* (Chicago: A. C. McClurg, 1909), p. 361.
7. Liang Yen, *Daughter of the Khans* (N.Y.: W.W. Norton & Co., 1955), p. 17.

MANCHURIA

MONGOLIA

Beijing

CHINA

I found myself with him. I was fairly bursting with the questions to which I simply must have answers.

"'Why have I big feet?' I asked him, my lips trembling to keep back the tears.

"'I told you,' said my father softly, 'the Manchus never bound the feet of their girl-children, and your feet are the natural feet with which you were born.'

"'But what are Manchus, and why am I one of them? Why are they such hateful people? Why don't the Chinese like them? Why aren't Manchus Chinese?'

"Very patiently then my father explained."[8]

The Manchu, Mongols and Chinese seem to have been different in other respects besides physical appearance. Until 1900 or so, education was not considered a major ideal for Manchu or Mongol women.[9] Upper class Chinese women were expected to read and write well, even poetically, but this seems not to have been an early ideal for Mongol and Manchu women. In the 20th century, however, Mongol and Manchu women struggled with Chinese

women to receive good educations and Manchu and Mongolian princesses opened schools for girls.[10]

Another difference between the Chinese and the Manchus is that the Manchus did not seem to practice female infanticide.[11] While sons were preferred, daughters evidently had fairly high status in the family and the respect they received from their brothers particularly might be high.[12] Manchu women also had some say in marriage arrangements. For example, sometimes Manchu princesses would decide to marry Mongolian princes -- life was harsher in Mongolia, but they would keep their rank as princess. If they married a Manchu noble, they would have to take his rank.[13]

When China became a republic, at first there was a drive to make all

8. Princess der Ling, *Kowtow*, pp. 45-56.
9. Even today the Chinese Communists claim that they have trouble convincing the peoples of upper Mongolia to place much emphasis on education. The reply the Mongolians sometimes make is that it is "bothersome."
10. Isaac Taylor Headland, *Court Life in China* (N.Y.: Fleming H. Revell, 1909), pp. 218-223.
11. Lady Hosie, *Two Gentlemen of China* (London: Seeley, Service & Co., 1924), pp. 264-269.
12. Carl, pp. 223-24.
13. Headland, p. 218.

Statues of women playing polo (c. 700 A.D.)

peoples accept the new Chinese ways. The Manchu court was disbanded; Manchu officials were removed from office; and Mongols and Manchus were told to take Chinese names. One Mongol woman partly resented this decision and partly felt a sense of relief.

"And I was bewildered and hurt... because of my name. I was only Jiaozhu, Clever Pearl. 'No Name!' the girls would shout with the scorn of people for that which they don't understand: 'Girl with no name!' My given name is Wuransubut, meaning pearl, and our family name is Barut, meaning willow.... These are Mongol names. I had been given a Chinese 'milk' or baby name, Jiao, meaning clever, which had been lengthened

into the 'book' name Jiaozhu on my entering school. But our family had no Chinese surname, and my Mongol surname was no name at all to my schoolmates.

"But the Republic soon afterward decreed that all of the peoples of China must bear Chinese names. Tibetans and Turkis and Manchus and Mongols were expected to become Wongs, Zhens, and the like. Father took the Chinese family name Yang, a translation of our Mongol surname. I then became Yang Jiaozhu. To my relief, I was no longer 'No Name.'" [14]

14. Liang Yen, pp. 19–20.

Woman member of the Inner Mongolian Equestrian Team

Manchu Princess in Traditional Butterfly Hairdo

When they came to power, the Chinese Communists promised to restore some of the cultures which were put down during the 1920's and 30's. But the Communists have felt a tension about minority groups and have feared too much ethnic identification. For example, Ghenghis Khan was either praised or criticized, depending on how easy the Chinese Communists felt about the Mongols as a minority group.[15] But while the Mongols are allowed their own "autonomous republic" within China and books are printed in the Mongolian language, the Manchus have no republic and are not encouraged to study their own language. Historians seem to have two views of this difference in treatment. One historian feels that the Manchus were so like the Chinese -- in speaking Chinese and accepting many of their customs -- that they easily fit into Chinese life so no special treatment was necessary.[16] Other historians feel, however, that the Manchus are being deliberately put down. The Chinese, they claim, have not forgotten that the Manchus ruled China and that they are politically able. Therefore, the Manchu culture may be a danger to the Chinese.[17]

What has been the effect of Communist China concerning Mongol and Manchu women? Official Chinese sources claim much progress for these women while they are allowed to retain their cultures:

"For example, a Manchu elementary school teacher recalled that before 1949 she had always written 'Han' in the 'nationality' box of her annual registration form because of the discrimination and oppression that prevailed in those days. Now because of the party's enlightened policies, she proudly entered the character 'Manchu'..."[18]

But little real scholarship has been published on these women and whether or not merely entering a name in a box means much is debatable. Until further scholarship is done, knowledge of the actual position of minority women in current Chinese life will not be known to the West.

Points To Consider

1. In what specific ways did Manchu and Mongol customs relating to women differ from those of Han Chinese?

2. Why might the Han Chinese children be especially nasty to the children of the Mongols and Manchus more than other minority groups?

3. Consider the following in speculating why the treatment of the Mongolian nationalities compared to the Manchu seems less harsh:

   a. Geographic location -- natural resources and industrial sites, and proximity to outer Mongolia

   b. Political leadership

   c. Population size

15. Dreyer, *China's Forty Millions* (Cambridge: Harvard University Press, 1976), p. 63.
16. *Ibid.*, p. 145.
17. Richard Diao, "The National Minorities of China and Their Relations with the Chinese Communist Regime," in Peter Kunstadter, *Southeast Asian Tribes, Minorities and Nations* (Princeton: Princeton University Press, 1967), p. 72.
18. Dreyer, p. 191.

Chapter 3

Women in Modern China

Chapter Contents

A. Attitudes Toward Chinese Women: Guomindang vs the Communists 1920-1940

"In the women of China the Communists possessed, almost ready made, one of the greatest masses of disinherited human beings the world has ever seen... and because they found the key to the hearts of these women, they also found one of the keys to victory over Chiang Kai-shek."[1]

Some historians have suggested that one reason the Communist Party led by Mao Zedong won, as opposed to the Nationalistic forces led by Chiang Kai-shek, was because of the attitude of women toward the two groups. Both the Communists and Chiang's allies had been members of the Guomindang. The Guomindang had supported women's rights and women's education. Members of the Party had gone to villages to change the traditional ideas about women. Bobbed hair became a symbol of the newly liberated woman.

But in 1927 Chiang took control of the Guomindang and ousted the Communists. The result for women was that while Chiang kept some of the measures formerly passed, he also developed a "New Life Movement" philosophy. This philosophy was sometimes at odds with previous Guomindang resolutions. While the "New Life Movement" had a Confucian emphasis, the Communists now relied more on Marxian views of women.

The following chart suggests some comparisons of this later Guomindang view of women and the Communist view of women:

1. What items seem more advantageous to women from the Guomindang's list?
2. Which items from the Communist list seem more advantageous to women?
3. If you were a Chinese peasant woman in the 1930's and 40's, which side would you have supported?
4. What other factors might enter your decision besides women's rights?

1. Jack Belden, quoted in William Hinton, *Fanshen* (New York: Vintage Books, 1966), p. 396.

Chart Comparing Views Toward Women

	Guomindang	Communist
Leader's Views	1. None of Chiang's "8 Principles" deals specifically with women.[2]	1. Mao Zedong had written a series of articles in 1919 on the condition of women. In later writings he also mentioned the need for women's equality.
Attitude Toward Revolutionary Women of 1920's	2. Allowed the killing of Communist women, approximately 1000. The number of women who were raped but not killed, is not known.	2. The Party is severely hurt by the attack, the remaining women and men were very bitter. They claimed some women were merely teachers and students, not Party members.
Marriage & Property Laws	3. 1931 Guomindang Code: a. Patriarchal family abolished. b. No arranged marriages c. Father keeps child in case of divorce d. Adultery punishable for either men and women. e. No official concubinage. f. Women could inherit property. g. Father's family got custody of child if both parents dead. h. Both husband and wife own goods, but husband manages them.	3. 1930 Communist Code: a. Patriarchal family abolished. b. No forced marriages c. Divorce available for both men/women. d. No legitimate/illegitimate children. e. Polygamy prohibited f. Marriages had to be registered.
Enforcement of Laws	4. No registration of marriage; no major attempt to inform peasants of law changes; urban people followed new laws more.	4. Began enforcing in 1930 in Jiangxi and later in Soviet Yenan. Some appearance of attempted enforcement, how deep, not yet known.
Ideology Philosophy	5. New Life Movement: Stressed "Propriety, Justice, Honesty and Self Respect." The Eight Principles of the "New Life" do not specifically mention women.[2]	5. Marxist-Leninist philosophy stressed the equality of women.
Education	6. Military training for boys, nurses training for girls. "Girls and boys need separate training." Senior girls take care of younger students; boys practice as clerks, telephone men. However, women's groups work against infanticide, footbinding, slavery.	6. Some training courses for women in leadership technique; mostly co-educational but some special classes in literacy for women. Groups worked against infanticide, footbinding, slavery.
War Work	7. Women should care for orphans, write letters for troops, provide medical care. Teach home management and literacy to other women. Work on sanitation.	7. Women needed on farms to supply Red Army; medical support to army, some as soldiers.
Primary Duty of Women	8. To care for home and children.	8. To become a good citizen/communist.
Sexuality Morality	9. Women should be "pure" before marriage. Nationalist army officially to act "civilized."	9. Red army soldiers to be "chaste;" rape punished by death.

2. These 8 principles are as quoted in: Robert Payne, *Chiang Kai-Shek* (N.Y.: Weybright & Talley, 1969), p. 161:
  (1) Regard yesterday as a period of death, today as a period of life. Let us rid ourselves of old abuses and build up a new nation.
  (2) Let us accept the heavy responsibilities of reviving the nation.
  (3) We must observe rules, and have faith, honesty, and shame.
  (4) Our clothing, eating, living, and traveling must be orderly, simple, plain and clean.
  (5) We must willingly face hardships. We must strive for frugality.
  (6) We must have adequate knowledge and moral integrity as citizens.
  (7) Our actions must be courageous and rapid.
  (8) We must act on our promises, or even act without promising.

	Guomindang	Communist
Military	10. Madame Chiang Kai-shek was honorary Commander of the Chinese Air Force. She stated, "Women must stay behind the lines in time of war and carry on men's work so that the latter can go to the front and defend the country."	10. Red Army School 1931-1933 enrolled 200 women. However only two women are known to have commanded troops, though hundreds served with the army in Women Guards, Women's Aid Corps.
Feminist Movement for More Rights	11. Not encouraged. Statement: "The meaning of the women's movement is not to annihilate masculine strength . . . nor is it to put an end to the grace of women's nature or evade . . . motherhood. The women's movement must cut out an attitude of antagonism of the sexes."	11. Protestors told in 1942: "Full sex equality within the Party has already been established." Stress should be on class struggle, though women's work among peasants should continue."
Mothers-in-law and Daughters-in-law	12. **Motherhood supported in** Chiang's speeches which stressed the respect given to authority.	12. Communists encouraged more independence from the family. Women should have "speak bitterness" sessions to air complaints.
Labor	13. Women leaders of the Shanghai textile union suppressed; some leaders shot. "New Life Co-operatives" encouraged women in small industries; child labor and women's wage laws considered in Shaghai.	13. Resolution of 1928 demanded 8 hour work day, equal pay, weekly day of rest; supported trade unions. Small industrial co-operatives formed.
Marriage Custom	14. Got rid of costly weddings, encouraged "mass marriages."	14. Simple, official registration of marriages.
Political Leadership	15. Madame Chiang Kai-shek was involved in some major decisions. Women excluded from the Congress of Representatives. No voting rights for women mentioned in 1936 Constitution.	15. One or two of every five leaders of each soviet had to be women. Women delegates to Congress about 30% in Jiangxi Soviet; women had full suffrage rights.
Land Reform	16. No push for reform	16. Land reform generally postponed; some promise that women might eventually share equally when the large estates were broken up.

Sources for Chart:
Chiang, Meiling Song, *China Shall Rise Again* (New York: Harper Bros., 1941).
_____ , *War Messages and Other Selections* (Hankow: China Information Committee, 1938).
_____ , *This Is Our China* (N.Y.: Harper Bros., 1940)
Croll, Elisabeth, *Feminism and Socialism in China* (London: Routledge & Kegan Paul, 1978).
Davin, Delia, "Women in the Liberated Areas" in *Women in China,* edited by Marilyn Young, Michigan Papers on Chinese Studies, No. 15, 1973.
deBeauvoir, Simone, *The Long March* (Cleveland: World Publishing, 1958).
Diamond, Norma, "Women Under Guomindang Rule: Variations on the Feminine Mystique," *Modern China,* Vol. 1, No. 1, January, 1975.
Han Suyin, *Birdless Summer* (N.Y.: G. P. Putnam's Sons, 1968).
Xie Bingying, *Girl Rebel* (N.Y.: John Day, 1940).
Kristeva, Julia, *About Chinese Women* (N.Y.: Urizen Books, 1977).
Payne, Robert, *Chiang Kai-Shek* (N.Y.: Weybright & Talley, 1969).
Price, Jane, "Women and Leadership in the Chinese Communist Movement 1921-1945," *Bulletin of Concerned Asian Scholars,* Vol. 7, No. 1, Jan.-Mar., 1975.
Snow, Helen, *Women in Modern China* (Hague: Mouton & Co., 1967).
Strong, Anna, *China's Millions* (N.Y.: Knight Publishing, 1935).

B. Five Women of the Modern "Heroic" Age

Introduction:

There are five women, particularly, who represent the women who lived through the terribly disrupting days of China from the 1920's through the 1950's. For that generation of people, the casualties were high from political conflicts within China, from the invasion of the Japanese and from the civil war between the Communists and the Guomindang. These five women all were in some way endangered by the era; by Japanese bombs at Chongqing; by Guomindang killings of women revolutionaries or by the hardships of disease and starvation on the Long March. They also all survived and became internationally known as women who worked for their country. But of the five, only two still have honor in China. The fate of one of these women is presently undecided, another fifth women now lives in the United States. What happened to these women suggests something of the conflicts of the period and also the difficult roles of women in it.

The five women who are probably best known in the histories of this era are: Song Qinling, Song Meiling, Ding Ling, Jiang Qing and Deng Yingzhao.

Female Leader	Husband	His Position
Song Qinling	Sun Yat-Sen	President of the Republic of China
Song Meiling	Chiang Kai-shek	Leader of the Nationalist Forces in China and later Taiwan
Ding Ling	Hu Yeping	Executed in 1931 by the Kuomintang under Chiang Kai-shek
Jiang Qing	Mao Zedong	Chairman of the People's Republic of China
Deng Yingzhao	Zhou Enlai	Minister of Foreign Affairs and Premier of the People's Republic of China

As the list above shows, four of these women were married to the most powerful men of the time, the men who led China. Only the third woman, Ding Ling, achieved fame without a husband in a position of power. Yet, the four women who were married to notable men were themselves exceptional women. Song Meiling and Deng Yingzhao had achieved some positions as leaders of women's reforms before their marriages. Song Qinling and Jiang Qing had revolutionary sympathies

64

Sun Yat-sen and Song Qinling

before they were married. Though their marriages put them in the background, both Song Qinling and Jiang Qing emerged later as politicians in their own right. This pattern of husband and wife leadership seems rather unique in the Communist Party as compared, for example, to the current Soviet Communist leadership in which wives are kept in the background.

These women were acquainted with each other in various ways. Two of them, Song Qinling and Song Meiling were sisters, but later became bitterly opposed. Deng Yingzhao, Ding Ling and Jiang Qing were all at Yenan together helping in the Communist resistance to the Japanese. Deng Yingzhao and Song Meiling worked together at Changqing when Chiang Kai-shek's government worked with the Communists against the Japanese. But while they knew each other, even worked together at times and all supported women's rights, they were divided by political conflicts. Brief descriptions of these women's lives may suggest the effect of these conflicts on the lives of many women of the time.

Song Qinling (Madame Sun Yat-Sen): The Quiet Protester

Song Qinling, like her two other sisters Eling and Meiling, was educated in the United States. Her father and mother were Chinese Christians who believed strongly in women's education and that women should use their educations to benefit China. Eling, the oldest sister, had been secretary to Sun Yat-sen, a reformer of China who was supported by liberal Chinese and American Chinese. After Eling's marriage into the powerful and wealthy Kung family, Qinling became Sun Yat-sen's secretary. They fell in love; he divorced his wife from his arranged marriage; and they were married. Song Qinling then became

primarily an aide to her husband. But foreign visitors found her to have strong interests in issues like child labor and bettering factory conditions.[1] She presided with her husband at many social events when he became president. This broke the old tradition of Chinese women remaining in the background. This policy was later followed by her sister and Chiang Kai-shek when he took power.

In 1924 Sun Yat-sen died. While he had not managed to defeat various Chinese warlords competely or to form a stable government, he had acted as a unifying force. The political party he had helped organize -- the Guomindang -- had recognized his leadership. After his death the party became split into two major groups, the supporters of Chiang Kai-shek and the Communists. Chiang moved first and in 1927 he and his supporters instituted what became known as the "White Terror."

Thousands of Communists or those suspected of being Communists were killed. Casualties among women revolutionaries were high; any woman with bobbed hair was suspect.

Song Qinling's reactions to this brutality was one of horror. She described to an American journalist something of the events of those days:

"One of these girls-- we all knew her in Hangzhou-- was disembowelled by Chiang Kai-shek's soldiers on June 21st in Hangzhou for saying that the Nanjing war lord did not represent the party or principles of Sun Yat-sen. Her intestines were taken out and wrapped around her body while she was still alive. Girls

---

1. Adelaide Anderson, *Humanity and Labour in China* (London: Student Christian Movement, 1928), pp. 46–47.

and boys were beheaded for saying what they believed..."[2]

She tried, often unsuccessfully, to save some friends from the killings. But she became even more bitter when her sister Meiling married Chiang Kai-shek shortly after these executions. Since her other sister Eling had also supported the Chiang marriage, Qinling became separated and estranged from her family.

Her next years were difficult ones. The Guomindang could hardly kill the widow of their revered Sun Yat-sen and the sister of their leader. But they could harass her, refuse to have any of her protests published and arrest or execute her friends, as in the cases of Liao Zhengzhi and Yang Jian, who seemed particularly close to her political views. She spent some of her time in exile, in Hong Kong, the Soviet Union, Germany, and then in seclusion in Shanghai until the Japanese came. During the war with Japan, she was united with her sister Meiling in Chongqing so as to show a "united front" against the invaders. But during the civil war which followed, her sympathies were with the Communists and she went back to Shanghai. She issued a statement in 1947 predicting a Communist victory in the civil war: "The peasants will support the Communists who give them land and lower taxes."[3]

When the Communists did win, Song Qinling became known as a hero. She was given various posts in the government; she was Vice-Chairman of the People's Republic, President of the Sino Soviet Friendship Association and in 1951 received the Stalin Peace Prize from the Soviets. She wrote essays supporting the Chinese role in the Korean War and criticized "American aggressors."[4] Her most recent writings have been about the need for more equality for women in China. Among her recommendations have been -- equal wages for men and women and elimination of arranged marriages.[5]

As both the widow of Sun Yat-sen and critic of Chiang Kai-shek, she became a revered figure in China. One foreign writer found that some Chinese, referring to the Song sisters, said that "One loves money (Eling), one loves China (Qinling), and one loves glory (Meiling).[6] As the "One who Loves China," Song Qinling has become something of a legend in the People's Republic of China. Modern historians, however, have found it difficult to show that she is now anything more than a figurehead, remote from any of the real political battles within the Communist Party.

Song Meiling (Madame Chiang Kai-shek): The International Symbol

Qinling's sister, Meiling, the one accused of "loving glory," now lives in the United States. Her home is with Eling's family, the Kungs, who left China after the Communists came into power. For Meiling going into exile in the U.S. may have seemed natural. She was educated here and spent much of her time during and after World War II pleading the cause of Nationalist China. For many Americans she became, more than any other person, the symbol of "Free China" fighting against Japan. She was the first woman to be invited to speak before an informal session of the U.S. Congress. More than her husband, she became the spokesperson for China's role in the war. President Franklin D. Roosevelt said about her:

"I never was able to form any opinion of Chiang in Cairo. When I thought about it later I realized all I knew was what Mme. Chiang had told me

2. Vincent Sheean, *Personal History* (N.Y.: Garden City Pub., n.d.), p. 45.
3. Helen Snow, *Women in Modern China* (The Hague: Mouton & Co., 1967), p. 149.
4. Song Qinling, *Struggle for New China* (Peking: Foreign Language Press, 1952), p. 337.
5. Song Qinling, "Women's Liberation in China," *Peking Review*, Vol. 15, No. 6, February 11, 1972, p. 6.
6. Ilona Ralf Sues, *Shark's Fins and Millet* (Boston: Little Brown & Co., 1944), p. 164.

Chiang Kai-shek and Song Meiling

(Wide World Photo)

(Wide World Photo)

Jiang Qing and Mao Zedong

about her husband and what he thought. She was always there and phrased all the answers. I got to know her, but this fellow Chiang -- I never could break through to him at all."[7]

United States government aid and money from private supporters came to the Nationalists partly because of the gallant image of China she portrayed. Particularly close to her were the "Flying Tigers" led by Chennault, a group of free-wheeling pilots fighting against the Japanese whose planes she helped finance. She became honorary commander of what later became the Chinese Air Force. At Chongqing, during the war, she anxiously watched the air dog-fights and had the officers immediately relay to her the results.[8]

Besides her war work, Meiling is also credited with the reforms she supported in China. Before her marriage she worked with the YWCA to better educational and factory conditions. When Chiang initiated the "New Life Movement" to "modernize" China, she pushed for sanitary reforms and went on inspection tours to encourage better hygiene and the care of orphans. She believed that women should get involved in charitable and war-time activities. Her own personal courage was shown when she and her brother flew in and rescued Chiang Kai-shek when he was kidnapped and held prisoner in Xian in 1936.

Despite her abilities, Song Meiling's attempts at reform were often stymied by other forces in her husband's political organization. While Meiling and her brother, Song T.V., formed one pressure group on Chiang, the Zhen brothers formed another. Her ideas about efficiency and quick action were in conflict with the complicated, and often corrupt, groups which had put Chiang in office.[9] The "New Life Movement" also tended to go back to Confucian ideas about the

subordination of women. While Song Meiling was a symbol of women's ability to the outside world, lesser officials of the Guomindang tried, by force at times, to keep their wives at home and claimed their "absolute obedience."[10] Exactly how strained the relations became between Chiang Kai-shek and Song Meiling over these issues is not known. One source claims, however, that when Chiang seemed to want to negotiate with the Japanese in 1943, she threatened to leave him.[11]

After the Communists took over, Meiling joined her husband on Taiwan, where she founded the Women's Anti-Aggression League. But in recent years she spent more and more time with the Kung family and now, after her husband's death, she lives in the United States. To the foreign reporters who knew her, she seemed a rather glamorous, demanding woman. She did not bring forth the sort of affection observers felt after meeting her sister Qinling. She did give energy to Nationalist China in the days of the Japanese aggression. As one American pilot said at the time, "She's the only man who'll show any action."[12]

Ding Ling: The Writer

Ding Ling is the best known woman writer of Communist China. After a harsh struggle to be educated, she became an author. With her husband, Hu Yeping, she joined the Left Writer's League in Shanghai which was critical of the slow changes being made by the Chiang government. Her husband was arrested and executed in 1931; his last letter from prison urged her to

7. Snow, *Women*, p. 160.
8. Sues, *Shark's Fins*, p. 155.
9. *Ibid.*, p. 167.
10. Han Suyin, *Birdless Summer* (N.Y.: G. P. Putnams, 1968), p.
11. Snow, *Women in China*, p.*169.
12. Emily Hahn, *The Song Sisters* (Garden City, Garden City Publications, 1945), p. 263.

Ding Ling, novelist

continue their revolutionary writing. She became involved in organizing factory workers and in the writer's league. In 1933 she was arrested. Partly because of her growing fame as a writer -- particularly for her book *The Diary of Miss Sophia* -- and because of her illness in prison, the government released her in 1935.

Eventually, she made her way to Yenan and joined with the Red Army. There she was involved in propaganda work. She wrote and directed plays which showed the Chinese defeating the Japanese aggressors. A very lively personality, she impressed foreign reporters with her dedication and involvement in the cause, even to neglecting her own literary skills.[13]

However, Ding Ling was not totally at ease with the situation in Yenan. She was rather at odds with other Communists for various reasons. One was her life style. The Chinese Communists were known in Yenan as being puritanical. Soldiers were supposed to be chaste until victory and the wives of some of the Communist leaders were strictly watchful of their husbands. Mao Zedong's second wife, He Zichen, for example had two women -- Lily Wu and Agnes Smedley -- banished for what she thought were improprieties.[14] Ding Ling was somewhat an advocate of "free love" and her personal life had involved affairs with various men. Furthermore, she also took the position that literature, while supporting the political needs of the country, could also reflect a writer's own individuality. A third point of conflict was that Ding Ling did not believe that the Communist Party was doing enough about women's rights. She pointed out that revolutionary Chinese women had paid a terrible price in the White Terror. She stated that more women than men, for example, had been executed in the "Hunan Purge."[15] In 1942 she criticized the Party in a speech, "Thoughts on March 8th,"

for not giving women positions of equal respect.[16]

Her conflicts with the "establishment" of the Party did not go unpunished. In the 1940's she was forced to recant and accept Mao's ideas that literature should be at the service of the Party. In the years that followed she seemed to follow the party line well. She went out and worked with the peasants and finally wrote a novel, *The Sun Shines on the San Gan River*, about peasant resistance to the Japanese. For this book she received the Stalin Prize in 1951 and was vice-chairperson of the writer's group. However, in 1956, when Mao began the "Hundred Flowers Campaign" to allow criticisms of the government, Ding Ling got in trouble again. Along with others like the writer, Hong Feng, she criticized the quality of Communist writing and claimed more individualism was necessary for writers. She stated:

"I do not oppose the writing groups and such organizations that we have now. But I believe it is wrong for a writer never to be without guidance. A writer is not like a child who cannot leave his nurse, he would grow independently. Because no matter how literary creation is guided, a work is created through the individual."[17]

13. Robert Payne, *China Awake* (New York: Dodd, Mead, 1947), pp. 381-387.
14. Helen Snow, *The Chinese Communists* (Westport, Ct.: Greenwood Publishing, 1972), p. 251.
15. As quoted in Earl H. Leaf, "Ding Ling, Herald of a New China," *T'ien Monthly*, Vol. V, No. 3 (October, 1937), p. 235.
16. George Brenton, "The Yenan Literary Opposition," *The New Left Review*, No. 92 (July–August, 1975), pp. 93-106.
17. As quoted in Yiqi Feuerwerker, "The Changing Relationship Between Literature and Life: Aspects of the Writer's Role in Ding Ling," in Merle Goldman (ed), *Modern Chinese Literature in the May Fourth Era* (Cambridge: Harvard University Press, 1977), p. 306.

The result was that she was "purged" in 1957. She was removed from any official position and her work suppressed. Her past work was looked at critically. One story, "When I Was in Sha Zhuan (Cloud Village)," was used to show how immoral her writings were because the heroine had been a prostitute. The unfairness of this criticism is shown by a reading of the story: the woman had been raped by Japanese soldiers, forced into prostitution and had escaped with information vital to the Chinese. The twisting of the interpretation of the story to show Ding Ling's "immorality" suggests the manufacturing of charges against her.[18] Imprisoned and tortured by the Red Guards, she spent 1971-75 in solitary confinement in a jail for political prisoners. In 1975 Ding Ling was sent with her second husband, Chen Ming, to a farm in Shanxi Province. Currently she is writing again and hopes to publish a new novel.

Jiang Qing (Madame Mao Zedong): The Adventurer as Communist?

Another Chinese Communist woman whose fate seems to be unknown is Jiang Qing. Unlike Ding Ling, who seems to have been forgotten in the People's Republic, Jiang's presence is still there. But she has become, officially at least, an *object of ridicule*. Cartoons portray her as one of a "Gang of Four" who tried to destroy China. She is often shown as the "Empress Dowager" pulling her strings to control people, or even, in one cartoon appearing as a blond, tightly dressed, foreign-style woman. However she is pictured, the obvious message is that Jiang Qing is a terrible woman. She also held more real power in China than any woman since the Empress Dowager.

Yet, until the 1950's she was not well known, even in China; except as the quiet wife of Mao Zedong. Like Ding Ling she had come from a poor family. After some schooling, she became interested in acting and was part of various drama and motion picture groups in Shandong, Qingdao and Shanghai. When the Japanese captured Shanghai, she went to Yenan. There, rather like Ding Ling, she was under some suspicion because of her former affairs and career as a movie actress. Jiang Qing, however, married Mao Zedong after the divorce of his third wife. Foreign observers to Yenan found her quiet, gracious and primarily concerned with her husband's welfare. There were, however, rumors that Jiang Qing had unfairly taken the place of He Zichen who had been wounded and suffered through the Long March with Mao. There was, from the beginning of her career, some hostility within the Party towards her.

Until the 1950's, Jiang Qing was kept in the background. Partly she was there because Mao did not give her a more active role. She did, however, do some work on land reform and the new marriage act. Her health was not good and trips to the Soviet Union for treatments seemed to do little. However, as Mao's power became threatened, she joined with him in the Cultural Revolution, 1966-68.

The Cultural Revolution was a shattering event for China. Mao and Jiang Qing used it originally to eliminate some of the tendencies they saw as preventing "real communism" from occurring. They objected to a growing interest in China's past culture, to an elitism based on superior education and to people like Xiaoping, the present vice-chairman of China, who wished to institute greater cultural ties to the West. The result was that the "Red Guards" of young people were encouraged by Chiang and others to rebel against their

18. "Ding Ling's 'When I Was in Sha Zhuan (Cloud Village)' With a Discussion by Yiqi Feuerwerker," *Signs*, Vol. 2, No. 1 (Autumn, 1976), pp. 255-279.

universities. For example, a good commune worker would be a better applicant for college than the student from a professor's family; grades and academic ability counted little. The problem with the Red Guards and their attempts at "leveling" society was that they also began to criticize the Communist Party structure. As in the "Hundred Flowers Campaign," Mao cooled the attempts at reform by closing off open criticism of the Party.

But for the next ten years Jiang Qing remained in power. Officially she was the Minister of Culture, but with Mao aging, she became unofficially virtually the head of the state. Many of those who opposed her, like Deng Xiaoping were purged. Her primary interest was, however, in the arts and their use to instill communism in the people. The posters of Mao and "little red books" of Mao's thoughts were everywhere. Literature became a cliche: whatever problem the actor in a story might have, the words of Mao would act as a catalyst for proper action. Old Chinese operas and ballets were banned and new ones like "The Red Detachment of Women" were created. But the "acceptable" operas and ballets were few, and Jiang's influence was to limit severely the range of Chinese art. In the field of movies, her influence was particularly devastating, "not one good feature film was produced."[19]

She did, however, in the ballets and operas, stress more of women's roles in the Revolution than had been presented before. In an interview with an American in 1972, she stressed the need for more equal pay and for the need of many reforms for women.[20]

In 1976 Mao died and Jiang Qing's power did not outlast his death. Hua Guofeng gained control of the Communist Party and had her arrested with three of her advisors. They have since been labeled as "the Gang of Four" whose backwardness has undermined China's need for industrial and cultural change. Jiang had circulated a poem that Mao had written to her in 1976,

"...In the struggle of the past ten years I have tried to reach the peak of revolution, but I was not successful. But you could reach the top. If you fail, you plunge into a fathomless abyss. Your body will shatter. Your bones will break."[21]

While Jiang's fate is now not known, she is believed to be imprisoned near Beijing. Certainly her fall from power seems to illustrate Mao's prophecy.

Deng Yingzhao (Madame Zhou Enlai): The Most Respected Woman in China Today

With Mao's widow in disgrace the reputation of Deng Yingzhao has risen. Visitors talking to the Chinese are often told that she is the most admired woman in China today. She, like her husband, Zhou Enlai, seem to have the gift for graceful political survival. People who knew them claimed that she was the more expert diplomat of the two.[22] While Deng is a firm Communist, the admiration towards her may stem also from virtues which seem to reflect older Chinese values.

The diplomacy for which she is noted is like the stress on tact and "saving face" which was part of Chinese tradition. Probably the most trying time for her politically was when she worked with her husband as Communist liasons to Chiang Kai-shek's government. She was able to work with Madame Chiang Kai-shek (Song Meiling) in training programs for women's war effort against the Japanese. After Zhou Enlai's death,

19. Roxanne Witke, *Comrade Jiang Qing* (Boston: Little Brown, 1977), p. 403.
20. *Ibid.*, p. 253.
21. *Ibid.*, p. 478. It now seems that Jiang Qing will go on trial in China sometime during 1980-81. It promises to be a "sensational" trial although Chinese leaders say she will not be executed if found guilty of treason. See: *Minneapolis Tribune*, July 8, 1980.
22. Helen Snow, *Women in China*, p. 252.

Jiang Qing pictured as a witch-like member of the Gang of Four

Deng Yingzhao was sent on various missions to carry on foreign affairs for the Chinese government. As one western diplomat said of one of her foreign missions:

"...They'll understand that the Chinese mean business, because if they didn't, they wouldn't have sent someone of Deng Yingzhao's stature."[23]

Like her husband, she managed to bridge the factions within the Communist Party and has remained in her various offices.

Another way in which she reflected Chinese traditional values was in her marriage. Married to Zhou Enlai for over fifty years, she and he seemed genuinely fond of each other. Unlike the rather bohemian early lives of Ding Ling and Jiang Qing, her early

life was spent working for the revolution first as a student, then as a teacher. Though she and Zhou Enlai were acquainted with each other in their school days, love was postponed until their marriage. Observers at Zhou Enlai's funeral noticed the deep emotion surrounding Deng Yingzhao's grief and the friends who came to comfort her. At Mao's death there seemed little emotion around the widow.[24]

Another aspect of her personality suggesting both traditional and Communist values is her courage. All of the women mentioned in this chapter experienced physical

23. Linda Mathews, "Zhou En-Lai's Widow Sent to Cambodia," *Los Angeles Times*, January 19, 1978.
24. Witke, p. 470.

Zhou Enlai and Deng Yingzhao   (Wide World Photo)

danger from bombings, arrests, or assassinations, but Deng Yingzhao is the only one of the five to have gone on the Long March. This escape of the Chinese Communists to Yenan has become a symbol of the trials the Communist Party went through. She suffered from tuberculosis, semi-starvation and the physical hardship of the journey along with her husband. She described what going without food on the March was like:

"...In the grasslands we were ten days or more with nothing to eat but grass. In Guizhou we were able to pick rice from the fields, but bandits had stolen our utensils and we had nothing in which to cook it. We were often hungry."[25]

She is honored as one of the approximately thirty-five to fifty women who completed the March.

But in some ways she has been a rebel against traditional Chinese values, especially concerning women. She described how she felt when she was fifteen:

"In this period [after World War I] I hated the old Chinese customs, such as arranged marriages and the unfair treatment of women, but I had no constructive ideas on how to correct this. I only thought that a girl must be allowed to earn her own living if she wanted an independent life and freedom."[26]

She refused an arranged marriage and worked hard to get the teaching and bookkeeping skills which would make her financially independent. In 1923 she joined the Beijing Women's Rights group-- and her interest in women's rights has continued to the present as a leader in the Communist Party, and as vice-chairman of the National People's Congress and vice-chairman of the National Women's Federation. She is frequently quoted concerning the need for further change for women in China.

25. Anne Louise Strong, *One Fifth of Mankind* (New York: Modern Age Books, 1938), p. 173.
26. Snow, *Women in China*, p. 254.

Helen Snow, an American writer trusted by the Communists, made a point concerning the differences in outlook she saw between male and female Chinese Communists. For the troubles of China, most males seemed to blame "everything from the peanut crop to American imperialism." Women are more inclined to blame China's troubles on poverty and 'the bondage of the feudal family.'[27] Because of this outlook, it seemed that women wished more "friendly relations with women of all lands." Deng Yingzhao, especially, has made this point to foreign visitors. The recent renewal of diplomatic relations between the United States and China were partly based on the outlook of Chou Enlai and his wife, Deng Yingzhao.

These five women came from widely different backgrounds and often had quite different visions of what China should become. But all illustrated a belief in creating a better China and a more just world for women and were personal examples of courage.

Points To Consider

1. Despite differences in political views, what things did these five women have in common?

2. Why did the two Song sisters, Qinling and Meiling, break apart?

3. Some of these women became symbols of various political ideas. What "symbol" did each of the following represent?

   a. Song Meiling (Madame Chiang Kai-shek) to the U.S. in the 1940's

   b. Ding Ling in 1957

   c. Jiang Qing in the late 1970's

4. The woman who seems to have most prestige in China now is Deng Yingzhao. What qualities in her seem to be ideals for Communist China?

27. *Ibid.*, p. 28.

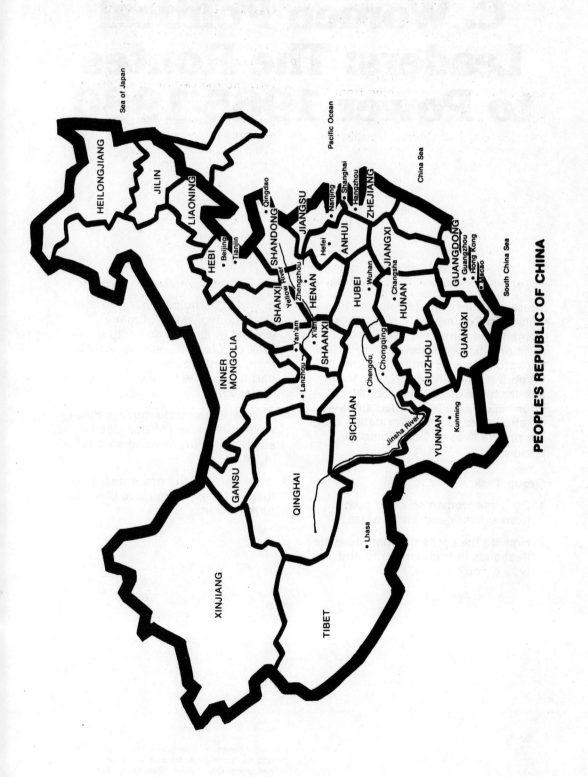

PEOPLE'S REPUBLIC OF CHINA

C. Women Political Leaders: The Routes to Power 1965-1980

There are approximately 400 million women in Communist China. Those women who have held important positions, however, have backgrounds with similar patterns. Using the following chart[1] (try to answer these questions. (Some information may be omitted since it is rather hard to find information on the private lives of Communist leaders.)

Group Task

1. Do these women seem to come from similar geographic areas?

2. How do their jobs compare to their husbands in both authority and type of job?

3. In what "participation" were these women involved? Not many women in all of China actually took part in these events. Why then, might women who had participated be so well represented?

4. What age group do most of these women represent? What does that suggest for future leadership roles in China?

5. What parts of the government do these women seem more likely to have jobs in?

1. Chart is based on information from a variety of sources, but particularly Barbara Wolfe Jancar, *Women Under Communism* (Baltimore: John Hopkins University, 1978) and Helen Snow, *Women in Modern China* (Hague: Mouton Press, 1965).

c. 1965-1980

Woman	Her Husband	Her Position	His Position	Place of Birth	Participation*
Kang Kejing	Zhu De	Chairman of Child Welfare; All China Women's Federation	Head of Red Army	Jiangxi (1912)	Yenan
Zhuo	Deng Xiaoping	Head of Government Office Answering People's Letters	Prime Minister of China	Yunnan Province	December 9th Yenan
Gung Beng	Jiao Guanhua	Director of Intelligence Ministry of Foreign Affairs	Vice-minister of Foreign Affairs	Hefei, Anhui	December 9th Yenan
Zhen Shooming		Member Standing Committee National Policy Council		Jinan, Shandong, (1905)	Long March
Jiang Qing	Mao Zedong	Member of Politburo	Chairman of People's Republic of China	Shandong	Yenan
Gung Busheng	Zhang Hanfu	Trans. Foreign Diplomat Zhou En-lai	Ambassador Ministry of Foreign Affairs	Hefei, Anhui	December 9th
Zai Chang	Li Fu-Zhun	Central Committee of CCP	Vice-chairman National People's Congress	Hunan, 1900	Long March
Zeng Xianzhi	Ye Jianying	Member Presidium Secretary of National Women's Federation	General	Hunan	
Wang Guangmei	Liu Shaoji	Worked in Foreign Affairs section	State Head; Disgraced		
Hu Liliang	Huang Hua	Vice-chief of Foreign Ministry	Foreign Minister	1913	
Li Zhen	Gan Siqi	Major General (1955) PLA Military Supply Officer	Army General	Hunan, 1910	Long March
Wang Zheng	Han Nianlong	Deputy Chief of Foreign Ministry Information Center	Deputy Foreign Minister		
Jing Buzhen	Liao Zhengzhi	Official in China Japanese Friendship Society	Vice-chairman National People's Congress Chairman Japan-China Friendship		
Deng Yingzhao	Zhou Enlai	Vice-President National People's Congress Head of various diplomatic missions	Standing Committee of Politburo	Xianyang Hunan, 1903	May Fourth Long March
Song Qinling	Sun Yat-sen	Vice-chairman National People's Congress	President of 1912 Republic People's Congress	Shanghai	
Li Bou-zhao	Yang Shangkun	Vice-president 2nd Chinese People's Consultative Congress	Magistrate	1911	Long March

*By participation is meant involvement in important political events:
May Fourth Movement (1919) — protests against Versailles Treaty
Long March (1934-35) — Communist escape to Yenan
December 9th (1935) — University protests against Japanese aggression
Yenan — World War II location of Communist forces

D. Peasant Women and Village Change

In 1947, during the Chinese civil war between the Guomindang and the Communists, two English sociologists, Isabel and David Crook, lived a number of weeks in a village in the area occupied by the Red Chinese. In the 1960's, they returned to this village -- Ten Mile Inn -- to study changes that had taken place since the Communist Revolution.

In this follow-up study of Ten Mile Inn, they begin by reviewing what it was like to be a poor peasant in the 1930's and 1940's before the Communist era:

"Before the land reform [1948] 70 percent of the people of Ten Mile Inn lived for most of the year on husks, wild herbs and watery gruel 'so thin you could see the reflection of the moon in it.' It was no rare thing for a family of five to share one ragged quilt, sleeping in a circle on the kang (heated brick bed), feet in the middle and heads out all round. In the very poorest families husband and wife might share one pair of trousers, to be worn by whomever went out.

"In 1942-43 in the midst of bitter struggle against the enemy [Japan] famine struck....

"For untold generations famine had been a regular feature of Chinese rural life. It had brought death and disease to millions and forced millions more into beggary.

"It had broken up families, forcing parents to sell, give away, abandon-- even kill-- their own children, rather than see them starve.

"The famine of 1942-43 was exceptionally severe and in adjoining areas under Guomindang administration the misery of the people was on a scale and of a nature which hardly bear description. The Communists, however, though they had only just established themselves in the Ten Mile Inn area, called on the people not to yield to famine as they had done in the past. On their initiative a militant peasant union came into being, which seized the hoarded grain of the landlords and rich peasants, cooked it in great cauldrons and served it to the hungry.

"But these efforts, especially in the face of the Japanese onslaught, had their limits. They lessened suffering. They could not prevent it. People still went begging, sold their children, hanged themselves. In 49 of Ten Mile Inn's 400-odd families, 59 people starved to death."[1]

It is not surprising that communism particularly appealed to the poor peasants who made up 70% of Ten Mile Inn's population. The Crook's information indicated (and numerous other sources agree) that the Communists showed greater fairness and concern toward the poor peasants than did the Guomindang. Perhaps these peasants did not really know what a communist regime would involve, but they did know that

1. Isabel and David Crook, *The First Years of Yangyi Commune* (London: Routledge and Kegan Paul, 1966), pp. 3-5.

Peasant woman brings tea in thermos to workers in the field 81

the Communist "cadre"[2] usually treated them with justice and tried to ease their sufferings with the famine.

This next life story illustrates how new leaders were found among the poor peasants. Guo Hengde was the first woman from the Yangyi area (where Ten Mile Inn was located) to join the Communist Party. No doubt the harshness of her early life influenced her decision to join with the Communists:

"Before Guo Hengde was born (in 1919) her father died, leaving his wife two mou of land.[3] For a lone mother and daughter to survive on that, in the landlord-ridden, warlord-ravaged Chinese countryside of those days, took strength of character. Both mother and daughter had it. As a child Hengde scoured the hillsides for fuel and carried back crushing loads. By the time she was thirteen she was a skillful spinner. When she was fifteen she married, but her husband was soon forced by poverty to leave for the far Northeast to try and scrape together a living.[4]

"...Meanwhile the young wife supported herself by needlework. When she was seventeen her mother died.

"Two years later, in 1937, news of the Communists' activities further up the valley reached [her village].... Following the Communist practice of relying on the poorest peasants, a woman cadre, named Guo Jing, found shelter in Guo Hengde's home. She ate the same food as the poor peasants-- husks and wild herbs-- wore coarse homespun cloth and spoke in homely language. 'We were soon like sisters,' said Guo Hengde. Guo Jing stayed with Guo Hengde two years and this close contact helped set the course for Guo Hengde's life....

"When Japanese forces drove through the area on mopping-up expeditions, Guo Hengde showed the communist cadres to secret caves, cooked for

them and hid their documents. When a landlord threatened her with death for associating with the 'red bandits' she was not intimidated. 'I never wavered,' she said. 'I knew they were for the poor. I would have given my life for them.'...

"In the same year she was elected head of a small spinning group, set up as part of the movement to fight famine by increasing production. Later she headed an 8th Route Army relief center, which distributed grain and cotton and saved 140 people from starvation. 'That was a terrible year,' said Guo Hengde. 'Over four hundred people left the village to go to Shanxi Province as beggars. But it was a bad time for begging. A hundred and twenty-odd starved to death. And here in the village it was the same. In Guo Da-cheng's family of five, two starved to death, one daughter was given away as a child bride and one son as a child bridegroom. There were suicides, too. Guo Ruzhi couldn't pay his rent so he hanged himself. His cousin scraped together enough to pay it, but then he had nothing left. So he hanged himself too.' In one family the husband wanted to sell the children rather than hear them whimper with hunger, but the wife threatened to leave him if he did. Guo Hengde gave them food saved from her own scanty meals and half a bushel of grain bought with money she had earned by spinning. This saved the marriage....

Guo Hengde helped young wives, too, to stand up to tyrannical mothers-in-law. In 1944 she was elected Spinning Heroine, First Class, at a conference of the whole Border

2. Communist Party workers on all levels-- later the term came to include government workers as well.
3. Women normally didn't inherit land, but there may have been some changes by 1919 or perhaps there were no male relatives to claim the land.
4. Nothing was heard of him for years as he did not know how to write and could not save enough to go home. The couple were finally reunited and brought up a family.

Workers on commune near Shanghai

Region. The same year she became head of the village Women's Association...."[5]

The Communist Revolution did not always guarantee liberation from male tyranny for women. Some Communist village leaders became bullies, just as wealthy landlords had often been in the past. Cases came to light in the early Communist government days, of women -- especially wives or daughters of ex-landlords -- being abused or even raped by Communist cadre.[6] In other cases women were forced to marry men against their will:

"Many stories revealed that [Communist] Liberation had not yet guaranteed free marriage or even the property rights upon which free marriage must be based. In East Portal one woman had been forced to marry a veteran. The cadres said, 'This man has fought for us many years. How could we live a peaceful life if it hadn't been for his efforts? We must reward him with a wife.'

5. Crook, *Yangyi*, pp. 16–19.
6. For example see William Hinton, *Fanshen: A Documentary of Revolution in a Chinese Village* (New York: Monthly Review Press, 1966), pp. 226–231.

When the woman refused, she was ordered to explain herself at a mass meeting.

"A second woman there wanted to marry a man from another village, but the local cadres would not give her a permit. Why make things difficult for themselves by further reducing the number of unmarried women?"[7]

However, after awhile these peasant women did begin to stand up for themselves. They ran for village political offices and became village leaders for the first time in China's history. They began to refuse to marry if they did not choose to and demanded property rights such as men had. At least under the new regime, these women did not have to endure the terrible deprivations so common to peasant life in China before 1948. The "Old Lady Wang" told her story to Communist cadre who had recruited her to work for the Party. Later she was elected a delegate from her village to a Communist Party convention called to suggest laws and policies for the new regime:

"The old lady told us how she had come from Shandong Province more than twenty years before, after her first husband had died. She, her mother, her brother, and her daughter ran out of money on the road. They had to sell the little girl for enough cash to continue. A buyer was found, but when the time came to leave the child behind, both the grandmother and the child cried so bitterly that the man thought better of the deal. He returned the child and gave the family enough wheat flour to last them a few more days. But tragedy trod the family's luck. Even before the wheat had been consumed, the little girl became ill and died.

"The surviving wanderers from Shandong finally arrived in the mountains of Shanzi as outright beggars. A distant relative arranged for Old Lady Wang to marry the

laborer, Wangshen, a man twenty years her senior. It was either marry or starve to death, so the handsome young widow consented. The match was ill-starred from the beginning. She was so badly treated by Wang's brother that her own mother and brother walked out one day in protest and were never heard from again.

"'I did not hate him,' Old Lady Wang said of the brother, who had long since died. 'It was the old society that made him cruel. In the old society everyone oppressed others.'

"'During the famine year I peddled beancake. My pants wore so thin that people could see my pi-gu (buttocks) through the holes and made fun of me,' she said. 'Now things are much better. We got an acre and a half at the time of the distribution and 30 bushels of corn and millet. We also bought half a donkey, and I got an old felt mat for the kang for five ounces of grain. The cadres didn't want me to have it, but I got it anyway.'"[8]

It's difficult to determine how much the lives of present-day peasant women in China have been improved:

--- Since no one owns farm property, all peasants live and farm on communes, there is no question of inheriting this property.

--- There seems to be evidence that village marriages are still often arranged with the help of a "go between" and the majority are still "patrilocal" marriages. Women are placed at a disadvantage because they move to their husband's village. *"They lack the local reputations and experience to earn them positions of responsibility and*

---

7. *Ibid.*, p. 398.
8. *Ibid.*, pp. 292–293.

84

Commune housing

***power. They lose seniority at
work.***"[9]

--- Pictures taken by recent
travelers to China show only
peasant women doing laundry
at country canals. It appears
that women still mostly are
responsible for "women's work"
such as laundry and house-
keeping.

--- Because of these household
responsibilities and childbear-
ing, their agricultural work is
less consistent than that of
men, therefore, they cannot
earn the same commune "work
points" as men. Other criteria
for awarding of work points
are physical strength and
experience. Again, these
criteria work against peasant
women. The accumulated work
points decide what benefits
from the commune are
received. It is tempting for a

wife to free her husband to
work towards more points, by
doing all the domestic labor
herself. Domestic labor does
not count towards work
points.[10]

Even though peasant women have
not achieved equality in modern
China, the gains they have made are
real. Women can participate in the
CCP and as village leaders. They are
not legally under the domination of
their husbands. Their mothers-in-law
no longer can claim their obedience
and labor. They can hope for a
reasonably comfortable life free of
the fear of unexpected disasters.

9. Judith Stacey, "When Patriarchy Kowtows: The
Significance of the Chinese Family Revolution for
Feminist Theory," *Feminist Studies*, Vol. 2, No. 2/3
(1976), pp. 92–93. See also: William L. Parish:
"Socialism and the Chinese Peasant Family." *Journal
of Asian Studies*, Vol. XXIV, No. 3 (May, 1975), p. 613.
10. Stacey, *Patriarchy*, pp. 91–92.

Woman farm laborer on modern commune

Points To Consider

1. What were the harsh conditions of peasant life in some areas before the Communists came to power?

2. What led Guo Hengde to become such a loyal Communist Party member?

3. Although the Communist Party did make an effort to help women, some of the cadre seemed not to have understood ideas on the equality of women. In what ways did some cadre continue to treat women as property?

4. In what ways does it appear that Communist peasant women still are not completely equal?

E. Status of Women in Contemporary Communist China

It is rather difficult to determine the current status of women in China for a variety of reasons. First, it has been hard for scholars to study the question because research areas have been closed to them. Chinese academic studies were severely curtailed by the Cultural Revolution and foreign scholars have had only limited access to sources dealing with Chinese women. Statistical studies in China have not been made recently and most of the data social scientists can find dates from the 1950's or early 60's. With almost a billion people, China has, of course, considerable problems trying to collect statistics. Thirdly, Communist countries, while supporting the idea of women's equality, have generally been opposed to independent women's political action groups. Without women within the country to speak openly, it is hard to obtain a fair picture of the state of women's positions.

However, some travelers, historians and Chinese officials have given observations from which some generalizations may be made. The following exercise may suggest some of these observations and the thesis they may or may not support.

Group exercise: Developing an Hypothesis Concerning Contemporary Chinese Women --

For this exercise, your group will act as a student who has been assigned a task of choosing a thesis and supports for a paper on Chinese women. Notes have been taken and arranged in two categories: 1) points that prove the Chinese communists have done very well by women; 2) points that prove China is still a sexist society. In looking over the notes, you find you have three possible thesis statements for your paper. These seem to be:

I. The Chinese Communists have made major changes for women and have only minor ways to go to real equality.

II. The Chinese Communists have made a few changes for women, but are still a male-dominated society.

III. The Chinese Communists have made major changes, but still have major problems to confront.

Your problem is to choose one of these thesis statements and offer proofs for your thesis from the items listed on the next page. On your worksheet, fill in your thesis, your major points and the items you would choose to support your points from the notes which appear on the following pages.

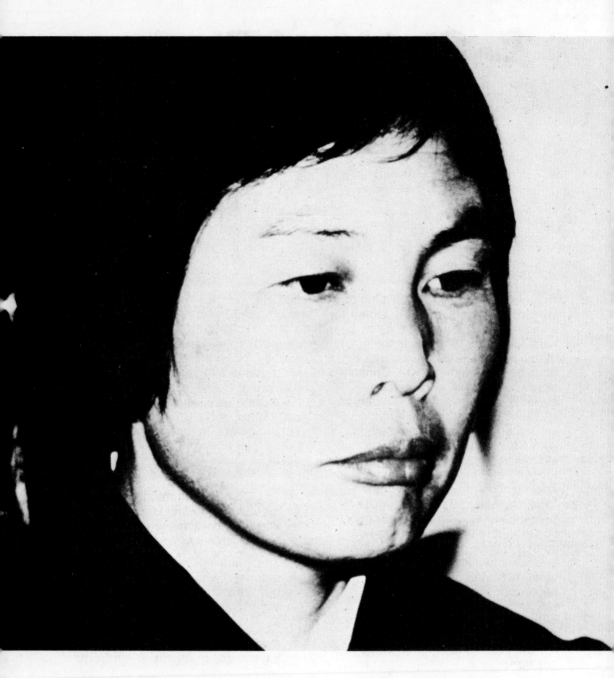

One of the Chinese women who act as interpreters for foreign visitors

Notes on Women in Contemporary China

YES, China has done well by women

1. Chinese women are in more occupations -- plant managers, iron workers, miners, pilots, doctors.

2. Women are paid more fairly for their work (for example, not the 12 hour, 7 day week, labor of Shanghai workers of 1920's).

3. Women got voting rights under 1954 Constitution, equal political rights.

4. Better medical attention, maternity leave, and birth control education are available.

5. Women serve in the militia; there are women military pilots.

6. Women have more chance at education; the literacy rate for women has probably increased dramatically; there is co-education.

7. Women are members of the Communist Party -- which holds real power in China.

8. Marriage laws are fairer (no arranged marriages; divorce allowed; no concubines).

9. Property rights are equal for women; women shared in the land reform act.

NO, China is still a sexist society

1. Discrimination on jobs still exists (all female elementary teachers, largely male truck/tractor drivers).

2. Women receive fewer "work points" than men (household labor not counted, more "physical" jobs get higher work points).

3. Few women, except for wives of officials, hold real political power.

4. The government controls birth control, encourages or discourages family size depending on governmental needs -- not by personal preferences.

5. Women do not hold high command positions in the regular Red Army.

6. Major universities enroll generally more male than female students. (For example, women are about 23% of graduates of Qinghua University.)

7. Statistics on women in the Communist Party vary, probably about 20%, and not in high level positions except for wives of major leaders.

8. Some marriages still arranged in countryside with bride price, still non-village marriages, divorce frowned upon.

9. Families generally pool their work points and father still makes economic decisions for the family.

10. Government writings stress that a girl is as welcome in a family as a boy.

11. Confucian ideals are criticized and seen as harmful to independent citizens.

12. Nursery child care should be available for working mothers.

13. Government writings encourage husbands to "help" in households.

14. Mother-in-law/Daughter-in-law relations are more equal.

15. Women's groups have been organized -- like the All China Women's Federation -- to deal with women's problems.

10. Rural parents still prefer boys, keep having children until they have a boy.

11. Respect and care for grandparents are stressed; "social security" measures for the old are limited.

12. Child care facilities are largely in urban areas and for children over three years; few facilities in rural areas.

13. Women seem primarily responsible for child care, cooking, washing.

14. Grandmothers have primary child care duties in rural China while wife works -- no "quiet" old age.

15. These organizations are formed by the government and may have been made ineffective during the Cultural Revolution. For example, the rather mild magazine *Women in China* was stopped from publication -- to be started again only recently.

Thesis on Women in Contemporary China

I. Thesis Statement Chosen: (I,II,or III)

  A. Major Point:

    Supporting Points 1
                      2
                      3
                      4
                      5

  B. Second Major Point or Minor Point

    Supporting Points 1
                      2
                      3
                      4

Bibliography of Sources for Status of Women in Contemporary Communist China

Chen, Pi-Cao. "Lessons from the Chinese Experience: China's Planned Birth Program and Its Transferability." *Studies in Family Planning*, Vol. 6, No. 10 (1975), 354-366.

Croll, Elisabeth. *Feminism and Socialism in China*. London: Routledge & Kegan Paul, 1978.

_____ . "Social Production and the Female Class: Women in China." *Race and Class*, XVIII, No. 1, (Summer, 1976), 39-51.

_____ . *Women in Rural Development: The People's Republic of China*. Geneva: International Labour Office, 1979.

Davin, Delia. *Women Work: Women and the Party in Revolutionary China*. Oxford: Clarendon Press, 1976.

Diamond, Norma. "Collectivization, Kinship and the Status of Women in Rural China." *Bulletin of Concerned Asian Scholars,* Vol. 7, No. 1 (January–March, 1975), 25-32.

Fu Wen. "Doctrine of Confucius and Mencius--The Shackle That Keeps Women in Bondage." *Peking Review,* Vol. 17, No. 10, (March 8, 1974), 16-18.

Goldwasser, Janet and Stuart Dowty. *Huan-Ying: Worker's China*. New York: Monthly Review Press, 1975.

Jancar, Barbara Wolfe. *Women Under Communism*. Baltimore: Johns Hopkins, 1978.

Leader, Shelah. "Mobilizing Half the Sky." *Far Eastern Economics Review,* December, 1973.

New Women in New China. Peking: Foreign Languages Press, 1972.

Orleans, Leo. "Evidence from Chinese Medical Journals on Current Population Policy." *China Quarterly,* No. 40, (1969), 137-146.

Sidel, Ruth. *Women and Child Care in China*. New York: Penguin Books, 1972.

Song, Ting Ling. "Women's Liberation in China." *Peking Review,* Vol. 15, No. 6 (February 11, 1972), 6-7.

Wall Street Journal. "For the First Time, China Encourages One-child Family." May 22, 1979.

Xu Kuang. "Women's Liberation Is a Component Part of the Proletarian Revolution." *Peking Review,* Vol. 17, No. 10, (March 8, 1974), 12-15.

F. Chinese Women in the 1980's

If the past forty years in China are any indication of the future, changes for Chinese women will be closely connected to the policies of the Chinese Communist Party. Though the ideology of the Party stresses the need for equality of women and men, there have been shifts in attitudes toward women depending upon other government action. For example, the prevailing views toward women were as follows:

1940's: **Involve Women in Land Reform and Party Activity**
This was the era in which women were seen as part of the peasantry needed to break landlord's hold on the land and to support the Communist Party against the Japanese and later, Nationalist forces.

1950: **Marriage Law Reform**
This reform helped women break away from patriarchal families and gave women the right to work and divorce. It also helped break down clan systems which might interfere with Communist village activity.

1956: **Great Leap Forward: Women Working Outside the Home**
This included Mao's attempt to get women actively involved in the work of communes, small industry and decentralized factories.

late 1950's: **Reaction Against Great Leap Forward: Back to the Home**
The economic failure of Mao's policies also pointed to the lack of childcare facilities and home disruptions caused by women working with no real family help at home. This era saw Chinese women's magazines stressing the importance of family life, suggesting cooking recipes, and supporting husbands in their careers.

1960's: **The Cultural Revolution: Women Back in the Labor Force, But To Assigned Jobs**
Women who had been too "bourgeoise feminine" were ridiculed. Wang Kuangmei, for example, was criticized for wearing a sophisticated black dress and pearls and was forced "to wriggle" into a tightfitting dress in front of her critics.[1] Another woman, sent as a barefoot doctor to the countryside, "felt she had lost ten years of her life and still felt like a country bumpkin."[2] For other women, the period of the Cultural Revolution was more positive. One interpreter describes, for

1. Victoria Graham, "Liu's Widow," Associated Press Release, March 3, 1980.
2. *China Update*, II, 2.

Crowd applauding visitors

example, how she gained self confidence when sent to Inner Mongolia. There she learned to ride, care for 1300 sheep and live in tents.

(From discussion with Ann Bailey, Midwest China Center, member of Community Metropolitan College faculty)

1970's: **Emphasis on Slow Gains: Growth in Employment, Child Care and Education**
After the Cultural Revolution, women's magazines began appearing again, stressing the need for more equality, but also including recipes. (See, for example, *Women of China*). The idea of women being a permanent part of the labor force was accepted.

These shifts in policies towards women are part of a pattern which sees women's issues as subservient to larger questions of foreign and domestic issues. While the Chinese Communist Party is committed to the idea of equality, it does have some problems in dealing with women's rights.

One of these problems is that it has trouble with the concept of sexism. Theoretically, if all economic injustices are removed, people ought to be equal. However, there may be in cultures assumptions about men and women that carry-over into their jobs. For example, Communist members have told tourists that it is only "natural" that women are grade school teachers and no men are; women "naturally" know how to care for children. The following statistics may suggest how job discrimination persists in China:

"At the 11th National Congress of the Chinese Party, August, 1977 12.1% of the Presidium were women 11.4% of the members and alternate members of the Central Committee were women. There were no women elected to the Politboro

* *

At the 5th National People's Congress in March, 1978 21.2% of the delegates were women

* *

In Hangchow, November, 1978 53% of the employees in the Silk and Brocade Factory were women. None of these was in the highest wage scale. One of the five directors was a woman. Three of the seventeen member Party Committee were women. A woman employee said: "We are not satisfied."

* *

Of the thirty Party members in a production brigade, three were party women.

* *

In Shanghai, November, 1978 Fourteen of the eighty-three doctors in the mental hospital were women

* *

The Chinese Ministry of Education released the following figures based on 1978 statistics (Beijing Review, Vol. 23, No. 1)

Girls made up 45% of the primary school enrollment; 41% of the middle school enrollment; 24% of college and university enrollment."[3]

While China, like the Soviet Union and other Communist countries, has increased the participation of women, some observers feel that women only reach "middle" jobs and never high level jobs.[4]

Another problem facing Chinese women in relation to the Communist Party is that historical women are not stressed and even the lives of current Communist women leaders are not disclosed. Minority groups and women in other countries have often felt it useful to look back in their histories to find heroes to model themselves after. The grave of Qiu Jin, the martyr against the Manchu, is neglected in China and other individual women are generally overlooked. The "hero" of the past then becomes the Communist Party, not specific women who represent a variety of points of view. A further problem with the lack of emphasis on historical women is that the strong women leaders of China now represent a dying generation. These women "paid their dues" in the Long March or in the December 9th Movement and have some respect among Chinese male leaders. When this generation of women is gone, there may not be another generation to replace them. This pattern has generally been true in other communist countries, where, for example, with the revolutionary generation women in the Soviet Union dead, there are no women serving in the powerful Politburo.

Another problem concerning the Chinese Communist Party and women's issues is the degree of freedom allowed women to push for their own views. Too much freedom or questioning may lead to arrest. For example, female activist Fuyuehua tried to protest a rape case and had encouraged a peasant rally

---

3. Ann Bailey, Midwest China Center.
4. See Barbara Jancar, *Women Under Communism* (Baltimore: John Hopkins, 1978).

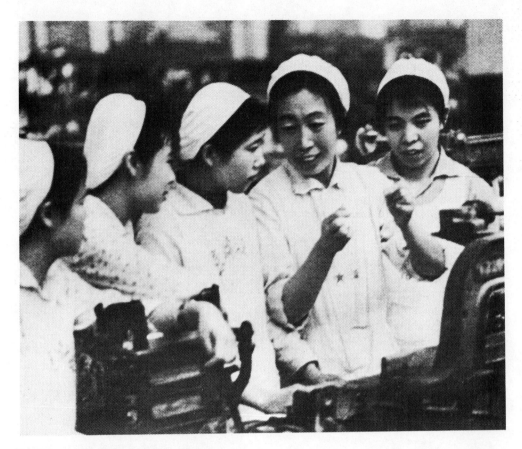

Textile workers in modern China

in Beijing's main square. She was arrested in 1979 as part of a crackdown on human rights dissidents.[5] While there was something of a "thaw" in the right to speak out against government policies after Mao's death, the Chinese Communist Party in the early 1980's seems to be moving toward greater control of public opinion.

There are in China today few signs that the past pattern of Chinese Communist Party policy will *not* continue. This pattern of change for women to fit into Communist Party policy seems to have brought most women in China benefit so far. Most foreign observers of China have found the women there as seeing a close tie between Party goals and

women's goals. Recently, a young Chinese woman responded to the question as to why she wanted to be a Communist Party member, "It's a great honor for me. But not only that, you know you are really helping."[6] Whether or not this sort of idealism about the Party will last depends on many factors -- ideology, economic problems, population control and foreign affairs. Real change has occurred in the history of Chinese women; it is difficult to predict what further changes are yet to come.

5. Minneapolis Star, October 18, 1979, "China is Cracking Down on Protests."
6. Ann Bailey, Midwest China Center.

Points To Consider

1. In which time period was the Chinese Communist Party most interested in specific reforms for women?

2. Why do you think Chinese women's magazines began to emphasize home activities like cooking and child care in the late 1950's?

3. What seems to be the present policy toward reforms for women?

4. In what ways do women in China today still appear not to have achieved equality? Even so, why do many women strongly support the Chinese Communists?

Women using bicycle cart as street store

Woman in center is chairperson of commune near Shanghai

Selected Bibliography

NON-FICTION

Belden, Jack. *China Shakes the World.* New York: Harper Bros., 1949.

Bullough, Vern L. *The Subordinate Sex.* New York: Penguin Books, 1974.

Croll, Elisabeth. *Feminism and Socialism in China.* London: Routledge & Kegan Paul, 1978.

_____. *The Women's Movement in China.* London: Russell Press, 1974.

_____. *Women in Rural Development: The People's Republic of China.* Geneva: International Labour Office, 1979.

Crook, Isabel and David. *Revolution in a Chinese Village: Ten Mile Inn.* London: Routledge and Kegan Paul, 1959.

Curtin, Katie. *Women in China.* New York: Pathfinder Press, 1975.

Davin, Delia. *Woman-Work: Women and the Party in Revolutionary China.* Oxford: Clarendon Press, 1976.

Goode, William J. *World Revolution and Family Patterns.* New York: The Free Press, 1963.

Hemenway, Ruth. *A Memoir of Revolutionary China, 1924-1941.* Amherst: University of Massachusetts Press, 1977.

Hinton, William. *Fanshen.* New York: Monthly Review Press, 1966.

Horn, Dr. Joshua. *Away with All Pests.* New York: Monthly Review Press, 1969.

Lang, Olga. *Chinese Family and Society.* New Haven: Archon Books, 1968.

Levy, Marion J. *The Family Revolution in Modern China.* New York: Atheneum, 1968.

Lin, Yao-hua. *The Golden Wing: A Sociological Study of Chinese Families.* New York: Oxford University Press, 1948.

Mace, David and Vera. *Marriage: East and West.* New York: Dolphin Books, 1959.

Myrdal, Jan. *Report from a Chinese Village.* New York: Random House, 1966.

Myrdal, Jan and Gun Kessle. *China: The Revolution Continued.* New York: Pantheon Books, 1971.

New Women in New China. Peking: Foreign Language Press, 1972.

Sidel, Ruth. *Women and Child Care in China.* New York: Penguin Books, 1972.

Smedley, Agnes. *Chinese Destinies.* New York: The Vanguard Press, 1922.

_____. *Portraits of Chinese Women in Revolution.* New York: The Feminist Press, 1976.

Snow, Helen Foster. *Women in Modern China.* The Hague: Mouton & Co., 1967.

Waln, Nora. *The House of Exile.* Boston: Little, Brown and Co., 1933.

Winnington, Alan. *Tibet: Record of a Journey.* London: Lawrence & Wishart Ltd., 1957.

Wolf, Margery. "Chinese Women: Old Skills in a New Context," in Michelle Zimbalist Rosaldo and Louise Lamphere, eds., *Women, Culture, and Society.* Stanford: Stanford University Press, 1974.

_____. *The House of Lin.* Englewood Cliff: Prentice Hall, 1968.

Wolfe, Margery and Roxanne Witke. *Women in Chinese Society.* Stanford: Stanford University Press, 1975.

Yang, Qingkun (Ch'ing-k'un). *Chinese Communist Society: The Family and the Village.* Cambridge: M.I.T. Press, 1959.

Yang, Martin C. *A Chinese Village: Taiton, Shantung Province.* New York: Columbia University Press, 1945.

Young, Marilyn ed., *Women in China: Studies in Social Change and Feminism.* Ann Arbor: University of Michigan Press, 1973.

BIOGRAPHY

Ayscough, Florence. *Chinese Women: Yesterday and Today.* Boston: Houghton Mifflin, 1937.

(Chao, Buwei) Zhao Buwei. *Autobiography of a Chinese Woman.* New York: John Day, 1947.

(Chow Chung-Cheng) Zhou Zhungzheng. *The Lotus Pool.* New York: Appleton-Century-Crofts, 1961.

DerLing, Princess. *Kowtow.* New York: Dodd, Mead & Co., 1929.

Hahn, Emily. *The (Soong) Song Sisters.* Garden City: Garden City Publishing Co., 1945.

Han Suyin. *Birdless Summer.* New York: G. P. Putnams, 1968.

_____. *The Crippled Tree.* New York: G. P. Putnams, 1965.

_____. *A Mortal Flower.* New York: G. P. Putnams, 1965.

Hibbert, Eloise Talcott. *Embroidered Gauze: Portraits of Famous Chinese Ladies.* London: John Lane, 1938.

Liang Yan (Briggs, Margaret). *Daughter of the Khans.* New York: W. W. Norton Company, 1955.

Pruitt, Ida. *A Daughter of Han.* Stanford: Stanford University Press, 1967.

Wales, Nym (Helen Snow). *The Chinese Communists: Sketches and Autobiographies of the Old Guard.* Westport: Greenwood Publishing, 1972.

Witke, Roxanne. *Comrade Chiang Ch'ing.* Boston: Little Brown & Co., 1977.

Wong Su-ling and Earl Herbert Cressy. *Daughter of Confucius.* New York: Farrar, Straus & Young, 1952.

LITERATURE

Buck, Pearl. *The Mother.* New York: John Day, 1934.

Chen (Jo-Hsi) Rouxi. *The Execution of Mayor Yin and Other Stories from the Great Proletarian Cultural Revolution.* Bloomington: Indiana University Press, 1978.

(Ho) He Jingzhi and (Ting) Ding Yi. *The White-haired Girl, An Opera in Five Acts.* Peking: Foreign Languages Press, 1954.

(Pa Chin) Ba Jin. *Family.* New York: Anchor Books, 1972.

Rexroth, Kenneth and Ling Zhung. *The Orchid Boat: Women Poets of China.* New York: McGraw Hill, 1972.

Seeds and Other Stories. Peking: Foreign Languages Press, 1972.

(Tsao Hsueh-Chin) Zao Xuejin. *Dream of the Red Chamber.* New York: Doubleday Anchor, 1958.

Glossary

Anthropology: (Anthropologist) The branch of social science that deals with cultural development and social customs of people. Often anthropologists study small groups of people to observe their social organizations.

Archaeology: (Archaeological) The science of studying prehistoric or historic peoples by analyzing their artifacts and other remains. Often involves excavation or digging up these remains at the site of an ancient society.

Artifacts: Any object made or shaped by humans.

Autopsy: Dissection and study of a body after death to determine such things as the state of health of the person upon death or the cause of death.

Boxer Rebellion: A rebellion led against Westerners in 1899–1900 that was secretly encouraged by the empress dowager Ci Xi . Foreign troops defeated the rebels and subjected China to many economic demands.

Bride Price: Money or goods paid to the bride's family by the groom's family.

CCP: Chinese Communist Party, members of which follow Marxist-Leninist ideas of socialist government.

Cadre: Various types of Communist Party and government workers at all levels.

Cash or String of Cash: A string of small coins strung together through a hole in the center of each coin-- worth a few pennies.

Chaste: (Chastity) Pure; not having had sexual intercourse outside of marriage.

Concubine: (Concubinage) A secondary wife who has some of the rights and privileges of a wife, but has less status than a regular wife.

Confucius: (Confucian principles or philosophy) A Chinese scholar and teacher (c. 551–497 B.C.). Though his life is surrounded by legend, the sayings and writings attributed to him form the basis of traditional Chinese social philosophy.

Courtesan: A prostitute who associates with men of power or wealth. Often known for their beauty and intelligence.

Cultural Revolution: A campaign (1965–67) that Mao and the Red Guards led against his "enemies." The term generally refers to the period in which intellectuals were under suspicion and in which Chiang Ch'ing (Mao's wife) came to have more power.

Daoism:	A Chinese philosophy or religion attributed to the probably legendary figure Lao-tzu who was supposed to have lived around the 6th century B.C. Started with the idea of attaining happiness by living a simple, natural life. In later Chinese history, Taoism became mixed with magic and superstition.
Dowry:	Money or goods paid to the groom's family by the bride's family.
Empress Dowager:	The widow of the emperor, who often was powerful in China as the regent for her son or foster son.
Eunuch:	Man who was castrated so that he would not pose a sexual threat.
Filial Piety:	A Confucian idea that sons and daughters owe absolute obedience to their parents (or in the case of a daughter-in-law, to her parents-in-law).
Gentry:	A class of well-off landowners of traditional China. They did not have titles as nobles, but were considered wellbred.
Guan Yin:	(Kwan-Yin, Kwanyin) The Buddhist female god of mercy in China who was prayed to particularly by women and sailors.
Guomindang:	A political party organized in China in 1912. It was originally a coalition of various groups who wanted a Chinese republic, not war-lord rule. In 1927, however, Chiang Kai-shek took control of the Guomindang part and led it until his death. After the defeat of the Guomindang by the Chinese Communists, the Party moved to Taiwan and ruled there. The Party was also known as the "Nationalist" Party.
Hundred Flowers Campaign:	A campaign started by Mao to open up the Communist Party to more criticism. When the criticisms became threatening to the bureaucracy, however, Mao closed off the speeches. Ding Ling was purged as a result of her comments in the campaign.
Infanticide:	(in-*fan*-ti-cide) The killing of infants.
Jade:	A semi-valuable, usually green, stone highly valued in China and used for jewelry and carvings.
Joint Family:	Practice whereby a group of people with a common male ancestor live together, share common economic resources, tasks and living space.
Kang:	Heated brick bed often part of a Chinese peasant home.
Kou tou or (Kowtow):	A Chinese custom of kneeling and then touching the forehead to the ground as an act of reverence or apology.
Long March:	Chinese Communists retreated from Chiang Kai-shek's army, moving from Kiangsi to Yenan in October, 1934 to October, 1936.
Manchu:	The name of a group of Northern invaders who conquered China and ruled it from 1644-1912 A.D.

Mongols: A group of Northwestern invaders of China who ruled China from 1279–1368 A.D. Inner Mongolia is not an "autonomous" region of China.

Matriarchy: (matriarchal) Where the mother is head of the household and descent lines are traced through the mother.

May Fourth Movement: A Chinese nationalistic movement that began with protests against the Allied powers after the Versailles Treaty gave Japan rights to Chinese territory. The height of the demonstrations were May 4, 1919, but the movement itself encouraged more questioning in not only politics, but also arts and social customs.

Natal Family: Family into which a person is born.

Nationalist Party: Another name for Guomindang forces led by Chiang Kai-shek who opposed the Chinese Communists.

New Life Movement: Chiang Kai-shek's program of reform in China that generally went back to Confucian ideas concerning women's household roles.

Norsu: A small tribal group located in the rugged Cool Mountains of southwestern China. Commonly called "lolos" (a derogatory term) by the Han Chinese, these slavers were feared by local peoples until the CCP persuaded them to give up their slaves.

Nun: A woman who is a part of a religious order and often lives in a nunnery or convent. Usually they are not married and often live a life devoted entirely to their religion.

Patriarchy: (patriarchal) Where the father is head of the household and descent lines are traced through the father.

Politburo: Ruling body of the CCP (Chinese Communist Party).

Polyandry: The practice of a woman having more than one husband at a time.

Polygamy: The practice of having several spouses at the same time.

Polygyny: The practice of a man having more than one wife at one time.

Pre-historic: History of people before recorded events and known mainly through archaeological discoveries.

Purged: Eliminated from all Party power positions and usually condemned as a traitor to Communism. Though not always jailed or physically harmed, a person who has been purged is often treated as an outcast.

Red Lantern: Women's divisions involved in the Boxer Rebellion.

Shrew: A woman with a violent temper and often having loud speech or temper outbursts.

Sibling: A brother or sister.

**Taiping
Rebellion:** A rebellion against the Manchu government in 1848–65. Women served in the armies of the Taiping, but in separate regiments. The rebellion was put down with the aid of Western troops.

Tantric Cult: A part of Hinduism (a religion of India) that stressed women's importance and the power of the female god, Shakti.

Uxorilocal: Husband comes to live with the wife's family.

War Lords: Military dictators who, using private armies, gained control of parts of China in the period before World War II.

Wet Nurse: A woman who nurses another woman's baby.

**White Lotus
Rebellion:** An uprising against the Manchu government in the 1780's, women fought with men. The rebellion was unsuccessful, but may have been a pattern for later rebellions.

White Terror: A term which applies to Chiang Kai-shek's attempt at eliminating the Communists in China in 1927. Communist-- or even bobbed-haired-- women were particular targets for attack.

Yin and Yang: A Chinese philosophy (a part of both Confucianism and Daoism) that there are two principles (Yin=negative, dark and feminine and Yang=positive, bright and masculine). These two principles influence the destinies of all creatures.

Explanation of Pinyin

The following is a reprinted explanation of the *pinyin* system of Romanization taken from: Molly Coye and Jon Livingston, *China Yesterday and Today*. New York: Bantam Books, 1979. pp. 360–362.

For one hundred years, since the time of the Western missionaries' first intrusion into China, Europeans and Americans have used a variety of conflicting and confusing methods to represent Chinese sounds. By now one set, the Wade–Giles system, has come to be used fairly regularly by American and British scholars, but it gives misleading and undependable indications of the true Chinese sounds. Twenty years ago the Chinese developed -- and in 1979 put into formal use -- a perfectly adequate system called *pinyin*.

The system is very simple. All vowel sounds are pronounced "pure," as they are in Latin. For instance, *ao* is pronounced to rhyme with "cow," *ai* to rhyme with "high," *ou* to rhyme with "throw."

On the following page is the official phonetic alphabet table published in Peking from *The Beijing Review*, No. 1, 1979.

A bit of further explanation is helpful toward understanding several sets of consonants for which we have only a single spelling and sound in English. For these the Chinese have two pronunciations and have thus chosen to use some English letters in unusual ways, as outlined below. We include these here in addition to the official chart because they are the most troublesome for English speakers. The letters *c, z, x,* and *q,* when used for Chinese, do not correspond to common English sounds, whereas the others in the table generally do.

Pinyin	English	Similar English Sound
x	sh	*sheet* (tongue lies flat)
sh	sh	*shock* (tongue touches roof of mouth)
j	j	*jeep* (*y* sound after j; tongue lies flat)

Pinyin	Wade–Giles	As in ...
a	a	far
b	p	be
c	ts'	its
ch	ch'	church[1]
d	t	do
e	e	*e* in her
ei	ei	way
f	f	foot
g	k	go
h	h	her[1]
i	i	eat; sir[2]
ie	ieh	yes
j	ch	jeep
k	k'	kind[1]
l	l	land
m	m	me
n	n	no
o	o	law
p	p'	par[1]
q	ch'	cheek
r	j	*z* in azure[3]
s	s, ss, sz	sister
sh	sh	shore
t	t'	top[1]
u	u	too[4]
v	v	*
w	w	want
x	hs	she
y	y	yet
z	ts, tz	zero
zh	ch	*j* in jump

Pinyin	English	Similar English Sound
zh	j	*j*aunt (no *y* sound; tongue points up)
ch	ch	*ch*unk (no *y* sound; tongue points up)
q	ch	*ch*ew (*y* sound after *ch*)

1. Strongly aspirated.
2. In syllables beginning with *c, ch, r, s, sh, z, zh*.
3. Or pronounced like English *r* but not rolled.
4. Or as in French *tu* or German *Munchen*.
* Used only in foreign and national minority words, and local dialects.

Three other letters vary from English; *z* is harder than English *z* and is closer to *ds* in "ads." *c* is equivalent to *ts* in "hats." The Chinese *r* is not quite comparable to the French *z*, as claimed; rather it is closer to the combination *r + zh* sound in Czech represented by *r*, as in the name Dvorak, without rolling the *r* too much.

The Chinese make only a few exceptions in their new romanization of Chinese words: Sun Yat-sen, China, and Confucius remain the same. But most familiar people and places now look quite different, even Peking and Mao Tse-tung. Here is a list of common new spellings with the old ones to the right.

Pinyin	Wade-Giles
women	**women**
Ban Zhao	Pan Chao
Ci Xi	Tz'u Hsi
Deng Yingshao	Teng Ying-chao
Ding Ling	Ting Ling
Guan Yin	Kuan-Yin
Jiang Qing	Chiang Ch'ing
Song Meiling	Soong May-ling
Song Qinling	Soong Ching-ling
men	**men**
Deng Xiaoping	Teng Hsiao-ping
Hua Guofeng	Hua Kuo-feng
Mao Zedong	Mao Tse-tung
Zhou Enlai	Chou En-lai
place names:	**place names:**
Beijing	Peking
Chongqing	Chungking
Guangzhou	Canton
Tianjin	Tientsin

About The Authors

Majorie Wall Bingham was born in Nebraska and received her B.A. Degree from Grinnell College and her M.A. and Ph.D. Degrees from the University of Minnesota. Her teaching experience includes being a junior high school teacher in Davenport, Iowa and an instructor at the University of Minnesota. Currently she is teaching history in the St. Louis Park, Minnesota, schools. Her professional activities include being a member of the Minnesota Council for the Social Studies Executive Board, on the Education Board of the Minnesota Historical Society and President of WHOM (Women Historians of the Midwest).

Susan Hill Gross was born in Minnesota and received her B.A. Degree from the University of Minnesota and her M.A. Degree in History from the College of William and Mary. Ms. Gross taught secondary English and history in Denbigh, Virginia, Savannah, Georgia and the Robbinsdale Schools in Minnesota before becoming a director of the curriculum project Women In World Area Studies. She served on the Robbinsdale Central Committee for student affairs, as treasurer of the Minnesota Council for the Social Studies and is presently recorder for WHOM (Women Historians of the Midwest).

Dr. Bingham and Ms. Gross have been invited frequently to lecture to various educational and community groups on issues concerning women's history, integrating women's studies into the curriculum and on issues concerning Title IX.